PEACEFUL DOG
MASTERY

PEACEFUL DOG MASTERY

A Conscious Path to Understanding Your Dog's Nature and Nurturing an Unbreakable Bond through Mindful Leadership and Non-Attachment

SASHA ARMSTRONG

Canine Behaviorist, Dog Shaman, Movement Leader and Entrepreneur

Acknowledgments

I extend my deepest gratitude to my grandmaster teachers, the wolves and dogs, whose guidance illuminates my path. To my ancestors and the Great Spirit, thank you for your unwavering support and the profound connections that inspire my daily life.

I am grateful to my animal and plant teachers for revealing the mysteries of nature and imparting their silent wisdom. To my spirit team, your protection and direction, channeled through the animals, are invaluable. I am humbled and forever thankful for the guidance and connections you foster.

This book reflects the lessons and bonds with all of you, for which I am immensely grateful.

An Introduction to Peaceful Dog Mastery

The inception of my 'Peaceful Dog Mastery' approach is deeply rooted in a lifetime of keen observation and empathetic understanding of dogs. Over the years, I've explored the intricate needs of dogs from various angles — psychological, behavioral, mental, emotional, physical, and environmental. This endeavor was driven by the recognition that, while many animal caretakers have good intentions, they lack the essential knowledge and tools to fully understand and cater to these needs.

Since childhood, I've had an innate connection with dogs, feeling and understanding their needs on a deeply personal level. This connection has allowed me to experience the world as they do, to feel their joys and their sorrows as if they were my own. It has been a journey of not just observing but deeply knowing the canine world from both the dog's and the human's perspectives. The path to developing 'Peaceful Dog Mastery' is complex and multi-layered. It transcends the conventional teaching of obedience; it's about fostering a relationship that benefits both dogs and their humans on multiple levels. This process involves understanding how we, as humans, can improve our mindset, energy, physical care of ourselves and our environment, and how we communicate. These aspects are crucial to truly appreciate the depth of our relationships with dogs.

My dedication to this cause started early. I've been working professionally with dogs since I was 14, and this lifelong commitment was born from a sense of urgency, almost a desperation that I felt as a child. Witnessing the neglect and misunderstanding dogs often endure was heart-wrenching for me. I was profoundly affected by how dogs experience this ignorance from the humans around them. Despite being surrounded by well-meaning individuals, the lack of attunement to a dog's true needs was glaringly apparent. This deep empathy and commitment have been both fulfilling and emotionally taxing. Throughout my career, especially during my twenties and thirties, I've had to take sabbaticals. These breaks were necessary for me to emotionally recharge and regain strength. The emotional burden of constantly being attuned to the unmet needs of dogs and the gaps in human understanding was overwhelming. But these periods of rest were not just times of retreat; they were also opportunities for reflection and growth, allowing me to return to my work with renewed vigor and insight.

Beyond Loving Your Dog: The Heart-Centered Connection

In exploring the shortcomings of traditional dog "training" methods, it's evident that current approaches often miss a crucial component – the heart-centered connection. This realization often emerges in spontaneous, serendipitous conversations I have, like a recent one while on vacation. I met a couple who felt they had manifested our meeting, indicative of the widespread longing for a deeper understanding of dog-human relationships. Time and again, I encounter people who have exhausted every conventional training tactic, from positive to negative reinforcement, without success.

The fundamental issue with these methods is their lack of understanding of the dog for exactly what they are, understanding their language, and meeting them exactly where they need to be met. Regardless of whether it's positive or negative reinforcement, the training often fails to establish a long-term, sustainable transformation in the dog-human relationship. It's not enough to want to bring positive energy and a healthy, vibrant frequency to our interactions with dogs. We must anchor these interactions in a heart-centered, coherent space, while also speaking the dog's language, which is essential for any meaningful relationship. People are generally well-intentioned and most likely already believe that they are connecting with their dog in a heart-centered way. However, being heart-centered doesn't mean that you love your dog. Most everyone loves their dogs. Heart-centeredness is about being centered within yourself. You love your dog, but you probably don't actually understand exactly who and what your dog truly is.

This lack of a dog-centered perspective in traditional training is glaring. The methods don't prioritize understanding the dog, their needs, and their language, nor do they consider how humans can embody the qualities of an effective alpha leader. Despite my extensive experience and open-minded exploration of various approaches since I began working professionally with dogs at age 14, this gap remains unaddressed. Now, at forty, my conviction in this regard is stronger than ever. There's a distinct lack of accountability, awareness, and responsibility in traditional methods, a failure to step outside our human biases to embrace the role our dogs need us to fulfill. My travels have reinforced this view, particularly my observations of dogs in communities with minimal human interference. These dogs are invariably more peaceful and content, a stark contrast to the behavior of dogs in more human-centric environments like the US or the UK. Discussing this with my brother, Seve, we concluded that our Western societal issues, particularly the rampant anxiety and mental health challenges, are being mirrored in our dogs. They are not just animal companions; they are barometers of our emotional and psychological states, often suffering silently under the weight of our collective problems.

Dog Shaman: Spiritually Leading, Healing, and Mediating Between The Human, Animal and Spiritual Worlds

In the mystical tapestry of life, our dogs emerge as enchanting and wise teachers, illuminating the hidden realms of magic and wonder. These mystical companions hold within them ancient wisdom and profound teachings, reminding us that we have everything to learn from their presence. Just like the Mystic who wanders in search of truth and enlightenment, our dogs embody a profound sense of curiosity and exploration. Through their playful antics and inquisitive nature, they inspire us to embrace the unknown and embark on a journey of self-discovery. They remind us to approach life with a childlike wonder, for it is through this lens that we can unravel the mysteries of the universe. In their eyes, we glimpse a depth of understanding that surpasses our human limitations. Their intuitive abilities, attuned to the subtle energies of the world, beckon us to tune into our own innate intuition. They guide us to trust our instincts, to listen to the whispers of our souls, and to navigate the labyrinth of life with grace and wisdom. Our dogs, with their unwavering presence, teach us the art of being fully present in the moment. They invite us to let go of worries, regrets, and future anxieties, and instead, immerse ourselves in the magic of the present. In their company, we learn to embrace the power of stillness and the beauty of simply being.

Our dogs are our mystical guides; as I incorporate shamanic practices into our endeavors it pushes us further into spiritual evolution and eventually a metamorphosis. Dogs mirror our innermost selves, reflecting back the lessons we need to learn and the aspects of ourselves that require healing. With their gentle guidance, they assist us in unraveling the layers of our being, helping us to uncover our true essence and align with our divine purpose.In their presence, we witness the profound interconnectedness of all things. They teach us that every being, every creature, holds a unique and sacred place in the web of life. Through their unconditional love and acceptance, they inspire us to cultivate compassion, empathy, and a deep reverence for all living beings.

Through my shamanic practice, I tap into ancient wisdom and rituals to connect with the spiritual essence of dogs and humans alike. By bridging the gap between the physical and spiritual realms, I am able to facilitate profound healing and understanding between these two beings.

As a Dog shaman, I guide my clients on a transformative journey of self-discovery and inner growth. I empower them to embrace their role as guardians and leaders in their relationship with their dogs. By nurturing their own spiritual connection, they learn to navigate the complexities of their canine companions' needs and emotions with compassion and clarity. One of the key aspects of my approach is the use of energy medicine. I harness the power of energetic healing techniques to support my clients in releasing emotional blockages and restoring balance within themselves. By healing the human, we create a ripple effect that extends to their relationships with their dogs and every other being in their life. Through my integrated methodology, I assist my clients in cultivating a harmonious and symbiotic bond with their dogs. By honoring the spiritual dimension within themselves and their Canine companions, they embark on a transformative journey of love, understanding, and mutual growth.

In "Peaceful Dog Mastery," I invite readers to embark on their own exploration of the spiritual and energetic dimensions of their relationship with dogs. I offer practical tools, insightful guidance, and inspiring stories to help them unlock the full potential of this sacred bond and create a life of profound connection and harmony. As we walk hand in paw with our dogs, we realize that they are not just our companions, but our mystical guides. They remind us that the greatest teachings often come from the simplest of beings. In their mystical presence, we discover that the journey of self-discovery and spiritual mastery is not a solitary one, but a sacred dance that weaves together the threads of our souls with the wisdom of the universe. In my book, "Peaceful Dog Mastery," I explore the interconnectedness of my shamanic practice, the understanding of our dogs' ancestry and language, as well as the mediation between the human, animal, and the spiritual world. These three elements form the core of my methodology, the Inner Alpha method, which guides my work with both canines and humans.

Confronting Skepticism in Compassionate Dog Education: Advocating for a Deeper Human-Dog Connection.

In my journey advocating for compassionate, conscious dog education, I frequently encounter skepticism, and at times, outright backlash. This resistance often reveals a deep-seated reluctance to challenge long-held beliefs about animal companionship and the human-dog relationship. One striking example that comes to mind is a comment I read on social media. It epitomized the mindset I often face: a dismissive attitude towards the idea of deeper understanding and empathy in our interactions with dogs. The commenter seemed almost to scoff at the notion of introspecting a dog's behavior, preferring to maintain a simpler, dumbed down, less involved approach to canine companionship.

This attitude is not uncommon. It stems from a perspective that views dogs merely as accessories to human life, existing solely for our convenience and pleasure. This one-sided viewpoint neglects the emotional and psychological depth of dogs, overlooking the mutual enrichment that a thoughtful, species-appropriate approach can bring to both the dog and the guardian. It's a mindset that treats dogs as passive participants in their own lives, rather than as sentient beings with their own needs and emotions. In contrast, the philosophy of 'Peaceful Dog Mastery' advocates for recognizing and respecting the intrinsic nature and needs of dogs. It encourages an honoring, respectful relationship where both the dog and the human learn, grow, and benefit. Despite these challenges, I remain committed to spreading the message of honorable, species-appropriate, conscious dog and human education. It's about shifting perspectives and paradigms, opening hearts, and fostering a relationship that goes beyond the traditional caretaker-animal dynamic.

Chapter 1:

The Issue with Traditional Dog "Training"

As we venture into the current state of dog training, a stark reality unfolds — a reality mired in outdated practices that are failing both our canine companions and us. At the heart of this issue is unconscious programming, a societal autopilot mode that dictates our interactions with dogs. This default mindset, deeply embedded in traditional dog "training" methods, is rarely questioned or critically examined, leading to a one-dimensional approach that neglects the deeper emotional and psychological needs of dogs. The conventional dog training lexicon — words like "training," "controlling," "curbing," and "owning" — is more than just vocabulary; it's a reflection of a mindset steeped in a loss of control and manipulation. This approach treats dogs as passive participants in their lives, reducing our complex relationships to mere transactions. It's a dynamic that's especially evident in methods like positive reinforcement with treats and clickers, where the dog's response is not born out of mutual respect or understanding but a Pavlovian reaction to a treat and a command.

Negative reinforcement also misses the mark. Trying to control your dog through tactics like dominance or correction seeks to control your dog to try and change its behavior, which not only is not effective but it doesn't honor your dog and it strays far from accomplishing our higher goals. These higher goals are having a relationship and bond that exists in a state of flow, balance, and harmonization. Where we aren't constantly demanding, fixing, or correcting. You should seek to achieve a state of being where less is more; where we aren't putting so much effort toward trying to make something happen with or for our dogs because this actually causes more harm than benefit.

Recognizing that dogs, much like humans, are opportunistic creatures is key. They respond to behaviors that offer tangible benefits. However, in most cases, this natural tendency is exploited without considering the dog's emotional well-being, and the relationship becomes transactional rather than transformative. This reliance on transactional interactions fails to foster a genuine connection and mutual understanding, reducing the bond to a series of conditioned responses. Oftentimes people are really coming from a good place. They truly love their dogs and want to do right by them but simply misunderstand cues like energy and body language. They humanize and anthropomorphize them, which creates a dissolution like smoke and mirrors to hide what is really behind their dog's actions, thoughts, feelings, emotions, and expressions. Those misunderstood cues are labeled as negative behavioral issues when they are simply missing the mark and not truly understanding what the dog is trying to communicate to them. Even without intending to dominate and coming from a place of true compassion, we can end up not providing the support or guidance our dogs need, missing opportunities to build trust and understanding.

In Peaceful Dog Mastery, we challenge these ingrained practices, advocating for a shift in perspective and way of being. We propose a philosophy that sees dogs as sentient beings deserving of respect, understanding of their intrinsic nature, and in relationship with humans that speak their language. Our approach transcends the simplistic treat-and-command dynamic, aiming to cultivate a relationship based on trust, respect, and a harmonious connection. It's about breaking free from the programmed responses ingrained in traditional dog "training" and establishing a bond that is actually real, which is enriching and fulfilling for both the dog and the human.

During a revealing conversation with a woman in Atlanta who aspired to be the "best dog handler she could be," I stumbled upon this startling linguistic realization. This widely used term, though seemingly innocuous, actually contributes to the underlying issue most Americans and humans across the globe are wholly unaware of. The idea is that dogs are simply possessions or beings that we are meant to handle, control, oppress, or use for our entertainment. It's precisely this mindset that we must fundamentally rethink. A lot of people don't believe they treat or project this mindset onto their dog but it goes beyond just language. Simply because you provide your dog with affection, food, water, toys, and a bed to sleep on doesn't separate you from controlling your dog. You might be inadvertently treating them like a possession even if you are approaching them with the best of intentions.

By the conclusion of our discussion, she experienced a moment of profound clarity, as if a lightbulb had suddenly illuminated her understanding. She had literally said, "Jesus, I never thought about it that way." Most people haven't and most people unfortunately don't. It's not because the issue is too complicated or that you need some sort of prior education, but that most people just don't even think about it. Most people are living their lives without pondering the words they use. The crux of the matter lies in our choice of language. The terminology we employ in discussing our dogs greatly influences our interactions with them. Persisting in using the term "handling" or all of the other commonly used terms implies a dynamic of control, suggesting an ongoing power struggle. Like us, dogs resist the notion of being perpetually managed. They also have their own sacred language and code.

Changing our language is key. It's not just about how we talk to or about dogs it goes beyond that. It's about the language that shapes our self-perception, influences our interactions with family and friends, and plays a crucial role in our professional engagements. Our presence in the world is shaped profoundly by who we choose to be. Our thoughts shape our language, and it's essential to recognize the power of words—they influence our creations and define our identities, ultimately determining what comes into existence. This cycle of thought, language, and manifestation proves the massive impact of our expressions and intentions. It's about communication, plain and simple. When we start refining the words we use, we transform the atmosphere of our interactions. It goes beyond mere conversation; it's about altering the energy that surrounds us. Such a transformation in energy invites us to hone our focus on the core values and principles that we genuinely hold significant. By embracing this deeper level of communication, we initiate a ripple effect, fostering new environments and relationships. This isn't merely about altering how we speak; it's about evolving our interactions to resonate with a more in-depth, purposeful frequency, thereby illuminating the aspects of life and connection that are most meaningful.

I can't impress upon you enough the importance of this distinction. Words have incredible power and they literally form the world around us. It's a philosophic understanding but it's one that has real-world effects and ramifications. Think about it this way everything that we understand and perceive is shaped by the words we've come to understand. There are a number of ways to explain this, but one particular example that aids in the explanation of this topic is when words are removed. Let's say that you were born on an isolated island removed from all humanity. You would be feeling incredibly alone, but if you'd never heard the term "alone" or had any other way to think about it, then it wouldn't even cross your mind that you were in fact feeling alone. When it comes to our relationships with dogs it is the same. If all you've ever known is that dogs are beings to be owned and that they are supposed to serve our needs, then you would have difficulty understanding that there was any other way to relate to them. This is what the Peaceful Dog Mastery Movement will achieve. The global community must recognize the profound contributions these remarkable beings can make. In order to come to a new way of relating to them we need to start using different language when referring to them.

The future of our journey alongside dogs isn't rooted in "training" them in the traditional sense or in any sense of the word. It's about fundamentally altering the language, the phrases, and the very structures we've constructed around these animals and their roles in our lives. It's a conversation that's all too rare—how do we show up in the ideal way for our dogs? This shift we're talking about—it's a complete unraveling, an unwiring of everything we've been programmed to think. I know this sounds like a massive undertaking and I'll be honest it is. But after decades of experience connecting with clients who've tried everything else in the traditional route, I'm here to tell you that it is absolutely necessary. Time and time again my clients express that they need to unlearn everything they thought they knew about living with dogs. This isn't about a few tweaks here and there; it's about questioning the very basis of our interactions with these beings who share our lives, and hold such a powerful place and significance.

The future I dream of demands a leap into a more sophisticated, respectful mode of interaction, where the language and actions we employ reflect a deep reverence for dogs as our teachers, not as beings to be molded to our convenience through harmful or unnatural methods. In this envisioned future, the language we use to describe our relationship with dogs undergoes a profound transformation, acknowledging them as the grandmaster teachers they are. This means no longer speaking of ownership or control, but rather partnership and coexistence. It's a shift towards recognizing the power of our words and ensuring they align with our true feelings of respect and admiration for these creatures.

The adoption of Peaceful Dog Mastery on a global scale will mark a paradigm shift towards a world resonating with higher vibrations of love, understanding, and interconnectedness. This isn't just about improving our relationships with dogs but about fostering a broader sense of harmony and well-being that extends to our interactions with other humans and the natural world. The ripple effects of such a transformation would be boundless, elevating our collective consciousness and bringing about a level of heart coherence that transcends our current limitations. This is the future I aspire to—a future where every interaction with our canine companions contributes to a more compassionate, harmonious world.

Chapter 2:

Understanding Pack Dynamics

Within the nuanced hierarchy of a dog pack, each member, from the alphas to the omegas, fulfills a crucial, distinct role. Alphas lead, betas provide support and act as backups to the alphas, subordinates adhere to guidance, and omegas often misjudged, play a pivotal role in sustaining harmony within the group. These roles are fluid; dogs adeptly adjust their behavior in response to the pack's evolving needs and dynamics. Whether due to the loss of a member or the introduction of a new one, the pack instinctively restructures, ensuring the continuity of each role and the stability of the group. The emergence of an alpha is driven by necessity rather than compulsion, a quality that is inherent rather than acquired. In the dynamics of the dog-human relationship, a crucial point becomes glaringly evident. Our dogs, regardless of their age — be it five weeks, five months, five years, or fifteen — instinctively seek a leader or leaders in their pack. They question who's in charge, and who they can trust, respect, and rely on. But often, they find a vacancy in this most critical role, a void in leadership that jeopardizes the pack's success and survival. These roles are deeply ingrained, echoing the natural inclinations found in human social structures, where individuals gravitate towards roles that align with their innate strengths and abilities.

In my professional experience, fostering this alpha energy in humans presents a significant challenge, as many do not innately possess these qualities. True alphas are a rarity among both humans and dogs. The common misperception that aggressive behavior in a dog park, for example, denotes alpha status is fundamentally flawed. Such behavior often betrays a lack of self-assurance and a state of distress, diverging significantly from the composed and secure demeanor characteristic of a genuine alpha's way. Drawing a parallel to the workplace, we wouldn't consider a boss or colleague who frequently resorts to aggression or loses their composure as embodying alpha leadership. True leadership, applicable to both humans and dogs, is defined by a grounded neutral demeanor and the projection of calm yet direct and aligned energy.

The truth is, that dogs are not inherently equipped to take on this leadership role in a world they don't understand. As humans we don't even fully grasp the world around us, so just imagine what it's like for our canine companions, who have been so far removed from their natural element and order. The essential components of a successful pack include leaders who manage, protect, and provide. Yet, in the vast majority of human-dog relationships, this leadership role is vacant, leaving dogs forced to fill a job description they are not naturally suited for. This misalignment is where much of the dysfunction lies. This absence of a clear leader in the human-dog dynamic leads to inevitable chaos. The dog, driven by instinct, feels compelled to assume the leadership role, as the pack's survival depends on it. In their DNA, woven into the very fibers of their being, dogs understand that without a leader, the pack is destined to fail. This instinctual drive is about more than just affection or treats; it's about the continuation of lineage, success, and survival. Dogs operate in a world of black and white — life or death, success or failure.

Humans, on the other hand, often dwell in the gray areas, leading to mixed signals and inconsistencies in communication with our dogs. This inconsistency breeds chaos and distrust. Consider the confusion a child feels when receiving conflicting responses from different parents — it's a similar situation with our dogs. They thrive on consistency and clear leadership, something that is most often lacking in our interactions with them. Dogs extend this intuitive grasp of social dynamics to their interactions with humans, perceiving and adapting to the energy and roles within a human family/pack. Human families are actually structured and function very similarly compared to that of a wolf pack. Dogs are remarkably attuned to any imbalance and instinctively strive to restore equilibrium within their 'pack,' be it canine or human in composition. Regardless of a dog's age, personality, breed, sex, background, or history, they are all hardwired to be aware of the need for the crucial role of the leader to be fulfilled. They will do their very best to assume it. Of course, the rare natural alpha personality will definitely find it much easier to fulfill the role, since it aligns with their inherent nature. However, this doesn't mean that they are immune to signs of stress, as they do need to fulfill their role in a world they don't fully understand. Dogs not suited to this role visibly struggle the most, as evidenced by their behavior in ways that are undeniable to humans. I want to emphasize that all dogs, regardless of how well they seem to manage the demanding role, experience these stresses. By deeply understanding their behavior, we will recognize that even actions not initially seen as problematic by humans can be indicators of stress.

This exploration into canine social structure reveals the layered nature of their instinctual behaviors, from alerting to potential threats to stepping into leadership voids when necessary. These behaviors are not arbitrary but are deeply rooted in the canine psyche, driven by the imperative of pack cohesion and survival. 'Peaceful Dog Mastery' seeks not only to elucidate these behaviors but to guide humans in engaging with their dogs in a manner that respects and leverages these natural instincts. Grasping the primal instincts of our canine teachers is more intuitive than one might assume. These instincts are a straightforward, innate language that dogs instinctively comprehend. For instance, modern-day dogs naturally bark at perceived threats as an alert mechanism for their pack or alpha.

In the traditional approach to dog 'training' — a term I use with much reservation — we see a myriad of incorrect practices. These methods fail to address the essential need for a united, coherent leadership approach, akin to the archetypal alpha roles observed in both human and canine societies. Whether it's in a family with single parents, same-sex couples, or any other configuration, the need for a clear, respectful hierarchy remains. Children, for instance, can be taught to assume a leadership role as it pertains to the Dog, understanding that being a leader is not about dominance or force, but about respect and boundaries. Children are actually better equipped to lead their dogs than the dogs are equipped to lead the children. Again, this is because we never want dogs to feel the burden of managing or being responsible for the child's welfare, as this can lead to undesirable behaviors rooted in stress. A dog can still be loyal and protectively sound, based purely on its raw instincts. Placing a stressful job description on a dog prevents them from acting from a place of grounded instinct. When in a state of high stress, their actions and behavior become erratic, unpredictable, and reactive. This is not the true nature of a dog but rather the behavior of an animal operating under moderate to high levels of stress.

Reclaiming Leadership: Restoring Natural Order in the Human-Dog Relationship

Grasping the intricacies of pack hierarchy is vital for resolving behavioral issues. Both wolves and dogs innately follow a structured social order, featuring the aforementioned alpha, beta, and omega roles. These roles are similar to leadership and subordinate positions in human organizations like governments, the armed forces, families, companies, and organizations of all sorts. This inherent structure is often neglected or misinterpreted by those questioning the relevance of pack dynamics in domestic dogs' lives. This is ingrained in the very essence of our dogs. Period. No matter how far dogs have come through selective breeding and domestication there is no way to remove their pack dynamics from their way of being. In other words, you can't take the wolf out of the doodle.

A typical scenario unfolds in homes with a dog and a couple, where a male dog will view himself as a contender against the male human for the leadership role. This perceived rivalry impacts the dog's relationship with the female human, whom the dog regards more as a mate, rather than a competitor for leadership. It's important to note that there can only be one alpha female and one alpha male. This situation can lead to dominant behaviors from the dog, such as occupying the male human's place in bed and displaying reactivity when this position is contested. It happens outside of the bed as well; dogs will try and claim space in many different aspects of our daily lives. These actions reflect the dog's attempt to affirm its supposed status within the family's social structure, which is a role that we have intentionally or unconsciously assigned to the dog.

This example proves the significance of acknowledging and honoring the natural pack dynamics that shape canine behavior. Recognizing these dynamics enhances our ability to communicate effectively with our dogs and tackle behaviors stemming from stress, anxiety, and confusion regarding their place in our households. By aligning our interactions and expectations with these innate social frameworks, we pave the way for a more peaceful and stress-free coexistence with our canine. Only once we understand that our dogs are trying to fill a biologically driven role, can we identify exactly why they are performing certain behaviors. Then we can take a step back and understand if we have given the dog a role it has no business undertaking. Once we can acknowledge that we can move toward reasserting a new pack dynamic where the dog can recognize a human as the embodied alpha Leader.

Reflecting on the thousands of transformative journeys I've witnessed, one particularly poignant, yet all too common, narrative emerges—a tale involving a woman, her dogs, and the archetype of a strained home environment. Her husband's engagement with their dogs is inconsistent, confined mostly to evening couch sessions, where he lavishes them with attention in manners that diverge from a dog's ideal interactions. This disjointed dynamic lays the groundwork for a home environment saturated with tension and discord. Burdened by solitude, the woman engages in endless dialogues with her dogs. They respond with barks to communicate their demands, such as the desire to venture outdoors or to be fed, not out of genuine need but because they've been inadvertently cast in the leadership role. This reversal of roles, with the dogs assuming the mantle of household leaders, stems directly from a lack of consistent and direct human guidance and clear communication in a language a dog understands. The dog, drawing from its survival instincts tries their best to assume the role of the alpha and believes that it is now responsible for the couple and their wellbeing.

Visitors entering this household are greeted with tumult. The dogs, assuming the role of their human pack's defenders, exhibit increased anxiety and defensive behavior, perceiving each newcomer as a potential adversary. The woman, meanwhile, often resorts to baby talk with the dogs—a practice more prevalent among humans than many would acknowledge—thereby reinforcing their authoritative stance. It's ironic how the human who is talking like a baby to their dog is really acting like the infant in the relationship. Although her actions are driven by affection, they inadvertently perpetuate this counterproductive dynamic. Most people don't understand that actions like this only further cement the dog's behavior.

This situation unfolds as a tableau of dysfunction. The dogs, viewing themselves as the protectors, are engulfed in stress. Stationed at the doorway, they serve as both symbolic and literal gatekeepers, regulating the household's ingress and egress. The woman's interactions, which inadvertently endorse their role as sentinels, further entrench their conviction that they must supervise and safeguard every facet of her existence, including mundane tasks like using the restroom or folding laundry. This setting, fraught with anxiety and inverted roles, is a far cry from the peaceful, symbiotic living arrangement we aspire to create with our dogs. The pivotal transformation required here involves the humans reclaiming their role as leaders, and restoring the natural balance where dogs are partners whose most important job is to trust their humans. In this equilibrium, dogs can relax, understanding they don't have elevated job descriptions to fulfill, and can trust in their human to handle those responsibilities, instead of acting as overseers or decision-makers. Embarking on this path necessitates the establishment of clear, calm, and consistent leadership, empowering the dogs to abandon their self-assigned duties and embrace their authentic role as lower-ranking members of the pack. Here a lower ranking member of the pack is freedom for the dog; it's basically the equivalent of a human being told by their boss that they can go on a permanent vacation. This transition is crucial for reinstating balance and tranquility, benefiting not only the human members of the household but also the dogs who depend on us for guidance and a sense of security.

People frequently misinterpret actions that seem problematic to us as mere misbehavior, when in reality, they are expressions of deeply ingrained instincts. Take, for instance, the common issue of dogs pulling on leashes. This behavior is a result of the mismatched role they are being forced to occupy. Since they believe they are the leader and decision-maker, they want to position themselves at the front of the pack. Consequently, a simple walk transforms into a mission for them, a hunt, if you will and they are the ones responsible. Dogs and wolves don't just go for walks. It's important to make this distinction that in their natural world, they don't perceive outings as leisurely strolls but as purposeful hunts. The dog is at the forefront, ensuring they confront any potential threats or make necessary decisions, such as choosing the direction or pace of the pack. They need to be upfront, that is their role. Anyone who has walked a dog will be familiar with this scenario. It's also worth noting that dogs naturally walk faster than humans. Our ideal outcome is to achieve a sense of fluidity and joy, as well as connectedness, during a walk or hunt, acknowledging that the dog has its own pace. We aren't forcing them to slow down and stay glued to our side, as that would be unnatural and overly controlling. We aim for connectedness - that is what makes an outdoor experience with our cherished dogs highly efficient, productive, and rewarding. I walk my dogs off-leash because I live in a vast, open area. My dogs alternate between walking and exploring ahead (but not too far), at my side, or behind me because there is mutual trust, allowing for a natural state of freedom in the time and space we share. The same can be achieved when walking a dog on a leash in a busy urban environment, where leashing is the safest option for various reasons.

This misconception is further reinforced by the rigid schedules we impose — walks at 08:00 A.M., 12:00 P.M., and 06:00 P.M., often following the same route. To the dog, these walks become their responsibility, a task where they lead the pack on a vital mission. They pull on the leash not out of disobedience, but because we have inadvertently assigned them the role of a leader on the frontline. Our journey with our dogs is not a pursuit of perfection, an elusive state by its very nature. Even the alpha, the epitome of leadership within the canine realm, embodies imperfection. The true hallmark of an alpha lies not in perpetual action but in the capacity to spring into action when absolutely essential, embodying responsiveness over-reactivity. This nuanced understanding of alpha leadership is often misconstrued, with many mistaking aggression or dominance as indicative of alpha status. This is unfortunately a misconception adopted by the dog "training" industry at large. Yet, authentic alpha characteristics are rooted in confidence, stability, and a direct approach, not in loss of control, overreaction, or domination.

Harmony at Home: The Impact of Energy and Narrative on Dogs

Initiating a transformative journey with our canine companions necessitates a significant alteration in both our approach and mindset. It involves a deep exploration into the narratives that have been etched into our consciousness, narratives that significantly shape how we interact with our dogs. These stories spun from our personal experiences, beliefs, and societal influences, play a pivotal role in defining the dynamics of our relationships with our dogs, which we have been in partnership with for at least thirty thousand years.

One memorable instance that perfectly illustrates this concept occurred during a visit to a couple's apartment in Manhattan. They were a very successful pair who deeply cherished their dog, a companion that had been part of their lives since his puppy days. Despite their deep affection and best intentions, the family faced a recurring challenge: their dog would become exceedingly agitated at the sound of the doorbell to the point of not only injuring itself but also redirecting his stress onto his family. It was a dangerous situation for all parties involved. Remarkably, the distress wasn't limited to the actual ringing of the bell. The dog seemed to react just as intensely to the mere anticipation of visitors, suggesting an acute sensitivity to its humans' thoughts. Whenever the family even contemplated the possibility of having guests, their dog's anxiety would skyrocket. This observation shows not just the auditory trigger, but also the dog's remarkable ability to pick up on its family's stress related to potential visitors.

Moreover, the dog began to associate the couple's phone with the introduction of perceived threats into the home. Any movement towards the phone would trigger a state of panic in the dog, who apparently linked the act of answering or using the phone with the door being opened for outsiders. This association turned everyday actions into a source of anxiety for the dog, who saw them as precursors to danger entering their safe space. This reaction was consistent, triggered by anything from package deliveries to friends visiting. It's important to note that, as has been the case for most clients over 20 years, this couple brought me in as their last resort. They had already enlisted the help of 10 other so-called professional "dog trainers," only to find that the issues and challenges with their dog were escalating and becoming increasingly intense—nothing had worked, leaving them completely devastated, powerless, and beyond stressed. This scenario is something I commonly encounter with humans and their dogs. The ongoing problems were putting a massive strain on their relationship and driving a growing wedge between the couple. The problem was so severe for them that they even relocated, hoping that would resolve the issue, but it was to no avail.

This situation was a clear indicator of an underlying issue. The dog, in his earnestness, believed his role was to guard the home, a responsibility that undoubtedly weighed heavily on him. The crux of the problem lay in the unspoken narrative we had all contributed to, casting the dog in a protective role he was not meant to play. The solution, therefore, was not to train the behavior out of the dog but to transform the narrative and energy surrounding it. In this moment of realization, it became clear that shifting our approach was imperative. Understanding the profound impact our perceptions and actions have on our dogs is the first step toward fostering a more peaceful environment. This insight led us to reconsider not only how we view our dogs' behaviors but also how we might inadvertently contribute to their stress.

Upon entering their home with a demeanor that conveyed the energy of the Embodied Alpha rather than chaos in response to a visitor, the immediate change in the dog's behavior was astounding. The couple was taken aback by the rapid dissolution of a problem that had been a part of their lives for years. The change occurred because of a number of factors. It was partly because the underlying story had changed. I was crystal clear about my intention, my energy, and my communication before I approached their home. I kept holding that vision and energy throughout the encounter. But there is more to it than that. There are many pieces to the puzzle of human-dog communication. The thoughts, narratives, stories, and energy which all come together to create the way of being. As well as speaking the dog's language and communicating with them in their own instinctual dialogue and code. All of these elements are what the dog is reading into and responding to.

This incident serves as a compelling testament to the substantial influence that a shift in perspective can wield. Our dogs inhabit the worlds we curate for them; by reevaluating our approach and the roles we assign to them, we can cultivate a new dynamic where the dog assumes a new role free of the stress of a perpetual guard or caretaker. Ultimately, the essence of this transformation lies in our perception and interaction with our dogs. A minor adjustment in our mindset can catalyze significant behavioral changes in our canine companions because it changes us. There's no necessity for extreme solutions like relocating or paying for endless "training" sessions. The key lies within us—how we define our relationship with our dogs, the roles we occupy, and the energy we introduce into our shared environments. It is within this realm that the true potential for transformation resides.

Understanding Defense Mechanisms in Dogs and Their Implications

The three primal defense mechanisms—flee, freeze, and fight—are not exclusive to dogs but are a universal language of survival embedded in various species, including humans and horses. This instinctual response system is hardwired into our beings, offering the best chance for survival by fleeing from potential threats unscathed. However, the complexity arises when dogs, constrained by leashes and navigating human-centric environments, cannot employ the 'flee' mechanism, leading to heightened stress and potential behavioral issues.

When a dog on a leash encounters a stressful situation and cannot flee, they might resort to freezing. This response, similar to the human reaction in confrontations where one feels paralyzed, reflects a state of panic and uncertainty. Depending on the individual's personality—be it a dog, horse, or human—this freeze response can escalate to the final defense mechanism: fight. The transition from freeze to fight is influenced by the individual's temperament, the personalities and chemistries of both dogs, and the nature of the threat. In the context of dog "training," misguided attempts to assert dominance, such as cornering a dog or using force, can provoke a fight response, especially in dogs with certain personality traits. This scenario shows the critical flaw in approaches that fail to recognize the dog's psychological state and resort to intimidation, physical coercion, or talking to the dog and praising it as a distraction trying to make a positive association. None of these are acceptable and they highlight the incompetence of humans using incorrect and species-inappropriate communication.

Prominent figures in dog "training," who advocate for dominance-based methods, completely misunderstand these fundamental aspects of dog psychology. By backing a dog into a corner in any given situation, they ignite the dog's fight response, leading to aggressive outcomes. Such confrontations not only endanger the human involved, totally compromising their consideration as an alpha but tragically misrepresent the dog's actions as inherently aggressive, overlooking the provoked nature of the response.

My extensive experience working with dogs, including those labeled as aggressive or beyond help, has shown me that understanding and respecting these defense mechanisms is crucial. By embodying the true essence of a leader—one that communicates effectively and respects the dog's psychological needs—I've navigated challenging situations without resorting to force or intimidation, and I have only ever been bitten a single time. After the thousands of interactions I've had with dogs, even those people labeled as aggressive, this is no small feat. This approach transcends mere dog "training;" it reflects a profound understanding of leadership that respects the individual's needs and boundaries. The real tragedy lies not in the immediate aftermath of such confrontations but in the long-term impact on the dog, who, despite "winning" the immediate fight, ultimately suffers the most. These incidents often stem from a damaged and wounded human ego trying to fill a void through dominance, similar to the harm inflicted by barbaric tactics on both animals and children. Recognizing and addressing these defense mechanisms with understanding is paramount in fostering a healthy, respectful, and fruitful human-dog relationship.

Navigating Stressful Situations: Understanding and Responding to Your Dog's Instinctual Reactions.

In discussing the nuances of dog behavior and human interaction, it's crucial to address a common area of confusion. Let's consider a scenario: a dog walking under a train track, with a roaring, thunderous train overhead. It's a situation that would naturally unsettle most beings — dogs and humans alike. To be unaffected by such a tumultuous environment would suggest a disconnection from one's surroundings. The intense noise and vibration are inherently disruptive. Dogs, with their heightened sensitivity, are even more prone to being disturbed by such stimuli.

Where the confusion often arises is in how people attempt to manage their dogs in these stressful situations. Many dog caretakers, misunderstanding their dog's needs, try to apply human tactics to alter the dog's perception of the stressor. They aim to transform a naturally stressful situation into a positive experience. This approach typically involves showering the dog with comforting words and treats in an attempt to soothe them. However, this method will backfire. When a dog is in the throes of a natural instinctual reaction to a stressor, like the overwhelming sound of a train, and the caretaker responds with consoling gestures and treats, it reinforces the dog's fear. The dog perceives the guardian's reaction as validation of the threat, intensifying their stress and fear rather than alleviating it. This also comprises the human's status or perceived status as the leader and protector.

In 'Peaceful Dog Mastery,' we address this disconnect and emphasize the importance of creating a neutral relationship with potential triggers. Instead of unwittingly reinforcing a dog's fear by acknowledging and reacting to it in a manner that amplifies the stress, the goal is to guide the dog calmly and confidently through the situation. This approach is about understanding and respecting the dog's natural instincts and sensitivities, and not imposing our human interpretations and reactions onto them. It's about teaching humans to become adept at reading their dog's cues and responding in a way that fosters confidence and trust, rather than exacerbating fear and anxiety. You can only do this when you truly understand the psychology of the Canine as well as the psychology and energetics of the human.

Chapter 3:

Respecting Silence: The Zen of Canine Space and Autonomy

Nashoba's Tale: A Journey into a Canine's Need for Space and Respect

Understanding our cherished canine teachers can be profoundly illustrated through the story of my German Shepherd puppy, Nashoba. This narrative embodies the core principles of 'Peaceful Dog Mastery.' From Nashoba's early days with me, I was intensely in tune with his needs and ways of communicating as I am with all of my dogs. This connection wasn't learned; it's a fundamental aspect of my innate understanding as a Dog shaman, focusing on aligning with their unique frequency and recognizing that the journey is centered around their needs, not mine.

Nashoba made it clear from the start that he valued his personal space and preferred not to engage with human-centric forms of affection. Honoring this, I respected his need for space, allowing our bond to develop in its own unique way. This respect for personal boundaries is a critical element of my approach as an embodied alpha leader, emphasizing the importance of understanding the role and its expression in our interactions with our canine teachers. After about six months of honoring his request for space and building our relationship within these boundaries, I gradually requested Nashoba to come closer. This transition marked a significant moment in our relationship, highlighting the impact of acknowledging and respecting a dog's personal space and boundaries. As the alpha leader, it is our duty to discern when and how to engage with our dogs in the most specific ways. We should always do so with a keen awareness of their comfort and consent, and setting the tone on our terms, not theirs.

In the broader context of human-dog relationships, it's vital to maintain a balance that respects each party's terms. We often unintentionally encroach on our dogs' personal space without considering their feelings or needs. Without realizing it, this respect for personal boundaries is not only relevant to our interactions with dogs but also to how we engage with children and others around us. The frequent disregard for our dogs' personal spaces, mostly occurring all day and every day, can range from mild to significantly intrusive, depending on the individual's approach and the specific dog and how they manage and deal with it.

This common oversight regarding personal space can provoke negative reactions from dogs, such as biting, lunging, nipping, and jumping up, often a direct response to repeated invasions of their personal space. Yet, many people react with surprise or offense to such behaviors, operating under the assumption that dogs should inherently welcome constant human intrusion, even when resting or in their own designated areas. This attitude reveals a significant misunderstanding and lack of respect for a dog's personal boundaries. It's sad really that we go ahead and label a dog's behavior as bad or say that the dog is acting out when in reality all it's trying to do is defend its own personal rights for autonomy and respect.

These signals highlight the need for human introspection and education on respectful mindful interaction with our precious dogs. To convey this concept to my clients, particularly those with children, I sometimes recommend demonstrating to their kids what it feels like to have their personal space encroached upon. This exercise is not merely about learning to respect a dog's boundaries but also about cultivating consideration, reverence, and an understanding of personal limits in all realms of relations. This real physical demonstration is incredibly useful to get the message across. Acknowledging that individuals who struggle with respecting their dog's boundaries may also face challenges in establishing and honoring their own personal boundaries is crucial. This is where real education and true guidance become invaluable.

Embracing Autonomy: The Power of Space over Constant Stimulation

Envision the goal of having a serene, well-mannered dog, a common aspiration among many. The ensuing query is: how do we actualize this ideal? The solution lies in valuing simplicity and practicing the art of restraint. It's about recognizing that silence is golden and, indeed, silence is strength. It involves giving your dog the liberty to exist without constant demands or a nonstop barrage of human dialogue and one-sided conversation. This entails, for a brief period, refraining from any requests of them beyond their essential needs. Provide them with nourishment, hydration, and necessary outdoor breaks, but otherwise, pause the regular regimen of activities and interactions. When we carry out these daily necessary tasks, such as letting them out, providing water, feeding them, and so on, doing so in this manner outlines clear communication. It illuminates the realization that our previous methods have been burdensome and unproductive, often causing more harm than clarity and thoughtful action on the part of both humans and dogs. It also allows for pure connection and for us to see how much of our time and energy is being directed at our dogs. This is a profoundly productive ritual to incorporate into everyday life with our dogs.

This minimalist approach, emphasizing autonomy and a respite from relentless stimulation, often unveils a profound truth to those accustomed to viewing dog training with skepticism or fatigue. For example, a partner initially apathetic or hesitant towards conventional "training" methods might find the idea of stepping back—offering the dog space without continuous interaction—a liberating discovery. Adopting this Zen-like, Daoist philosophy, which values non-attachment and reduces constant direct engagement, challenges the ingrained belief that more involvement, more "training", and more hands-on actions yield superior outcomes. However, in the context of building healthy relationships with our dogs, the reverse is true. Granting them independence and space isn't neglect; it's a profound respect for their individuality, creating an environment where they can thrive on their own terms. This revelation, that embracing minimalism and non-direct engagement can be incredibly effective, comes as a pleasant surprise. Thus, when pondering, "How do we achieve this? How do we shape a tranquil, equitable partnership with our beloved dogs?" The answer might very well be found in the timeless principle of 'less is more.' It's about recognizing that the space and autonomy we offer are the keystones to forging a deeper, more resonant connection with our cherished dogs, underlining the essential truth that in simplicity and space, we find the path to a harmonious life together.

Physical Touch and Affection: Understanding Boundaries and Respect

The nuances of physical touch and companionship stretch well beyond the bounds of simple human affection. For dogs, these forms of interaction are deeply embedded in recognizing their boundaries, respecting their personal space, and engaging with them in a manner that acknowledges and celebrates their uniqueness. It's crucial for individuals to thoughtfully navigate the nuances of how, why, when, and where they engage in physical contact and interaction with their dogs. Although dogs may relish the comfort of a soothing massage or specific kinds of touch, such gestures should always be guided by a keen sensitivity to the dog's comfort level and openness to the interaction. There are specific ways to touch and not to touch a dog but every dog is different and there isn't a complete one-size-fits-all approach. Start asking yourself questions. Is it okay if our dog doesn't want to be touched right now? Can I make a better impact on my dog by refraining from direct physical touch and engagement at this time?

We need to be discerning, which takes a heightened awareness, attunement, and a strong will to shift our go-to behaviors to a way of being that our dog honors most. Just watch how your dog responds to you when you show up this way- the proof is in the pudding. This mindful approach is close to how we might interact with children, or any living being for that matter, highlighting the importance of not imposing on them responsibilities or expectations that exceed their abilities. In a similar vein, placing emotional burdens on dogs that they're ill-equipped to manage can be just as harmful. Recognizing and alleviating this pressure stands out as one of the most meaningful expressions of our love and respect for our canine teachers.

A key part of this understanding involves reassessing our actions and the energy we emit. For example, the volume of spoken words we direct at our dogs is way more than they can process. Dogs do not have the ability to articulate through language the way humans can, however, they clearly articulate through their body language, postures, gestures, and energy. If a dog desires their own personal space or a quiet moment they can't tell you with words but they can show you through their actions. Many caretakers are taken aback when they realize the intensity of their constant verbal interactions with their dogs. Many people are completely unaware, asleep at the wheel, when it comes to observing and being attuned to what works and what doesn't for their dogs. Interestingly enough, many individuals completely misinterpret their dogs' response to physical engagement, often thinking it's cute and that they are enjoying it, or that they want it because the dog is intensely demanding it through their direct communication and actions. Opting for a day of serene cohabitation—immersing ourselves in our tasks while granting our dogs the liberty to just exist—reflects a deep respect for their need for peace and quiet.

The Embodied Alpha Election Process I advocate for is crafted to inspire a shift in human presence and behavior towards our dogs and in life and relationships in general. The goal is to become non-reliant on verbal cues entirely except to make an impact when it's absolutely necessary. The first step in this process is to gradually move away from relying on direct verbal interaction, focusing instead on connecting with our dogs through our energy and body language. This approach is much closer to their natural form of communication—the language that they inherently understand. Have you ever met a dog that spoke English? While the question may sound silly, it's surprisingly relevant. Many people believe their dog understands English, but what's actually happening is a form of a Pavlovian response. Dogs learn to associate and identify words with specific objects, situations, people, or environments through consistent repetition. They are absolute masters of association. They're always connecting the dots, figuring out how to respond to our cues to get something they need. It goes beyond needs as well where they do it simply because we respond to it, which can lock in an unproductive way of serving them. By acknowledging this, we understand that dogs do the best with the information we give them, highlighting the importance of our role in shaping their understanding and behavior. This adjustment can transform the dynamic between the dog and the family/pack. By reducing our constant verbal input, we open up a space for dogs to see us in a new light, valuing our company not for the ceaseless attention or commands but for our aura of independence and tranquility. We want our dogs to choose to be in our company and not feel that they need to be glued to our side, sitting perched on top of us as we try to cook dinner or sit on the couch. Have you ever noticed that your dogs make a massive effort to jump on the couch or your bed first? Have you noticed your dog racing up the stairs ahead of you to look down at you atop the stairs? These are just a few of the many not-so-subtle communications that the dog is showing us their belief in where they stand in the relationship.

This recalibration can tremendously affect a dog's state of well-being. Living under constant stress is as damaging for dogs as it is for humans. Our strategy doesn't strive for an unattainable stress-free ideal but rather acknowledges the presence of stress while being keenly conscious of our actions and energy. It's designed to navigate the wave of everyday life stressors. Stress will always be present; what's most important, and one of the many purposes behind Peaceful Dog Mastery, is that we ride the wave of stress with ease and grace when it arises. We learn from those challenging moments and are grateful for the beautiful lessons they can afford us.

A prime example of miscommunication in human-canine interactions is seen in how some individuals interact with dogs, particularly puppies, often driven by a transient wish for personal gratification, overlooking the dog's comfort and viewpoint. This calls attention to the need for a more thoughtful and enlightened approach to relating with our beloved dogs. An instance highlighting the importance of boundary respect occurs when puppies on leashes are approached by strangers, where the encroachment into the puppy's space can understandably cause stress and confusion. Would you allow a stranger to approach your baby in a stroller or your young toddler walking down the street? When you think about it, would you even want a stranger invading your personal space as you walk down the street? There's not a chance, right? Such inconsiderate actions, driven more by human whims than by regard for the dog's well-being, most likely leave a lasting negative impact on the young dog, shaping its future reactions and attitudes towards unfamiliar individuals and humans in general.

Recognizing and respecting these boundaries is a critical element of communicating in a dog's language, ensuring that our interactions contribute positively to their emotional health and safety. It's super important to note that under no circumstances is it acceptable for a stranger to approach your puppy or dog, talk to it, and touch it. A complete misunderstanding arises when people assume that just because the puppy is "friendly," it wants to make friends with everyone. This is absolutely not the case. Remember, our dogs do the best with the information we give them, and so they respond in a conditioned way. If you have a dog with an even-keeled nature or a friendly dog and you allow strangers to approach it, you might get away with it for a little while. However, eventually, your perfect pup may start acting out in response to being forced to deal with strangers all the time, doing their absolute best with the situation at hand. I see manifestations of this all the time; it's constant. Defense mechanisms arise as a result of the pressure and stress, and then it's the dog's fault for not being well-mannered and allowing such invasions of space. They're expected to sit there, be good dogs, and allow it, which goes way beyond what's fair in terms of honoring and respecting the species, man's best friend. I see plenty of dogs in very bad shape from these practices. The dysfunction it causes in their behavior and spirit is something I deal closely with every day.

Chapter 4:

Leading with Trust: The Essential Guide to Dog Leadership

Cultivating Trust: Consistent Leadership and Meeting a Dog's Needs

The path to forging a robust, trust-based rapport with our dogs is significantly anchored in consistency. This entails reliably being present for your dog in a manner that nurtures credibility, enabling your dog to develop an affinity for you driven by choice, not through manipulation, pressure, or a constant Pavlovian response. In a world enamored with gadgets, treats, and diversions, these elements inevitably influence our canine, often mirroring our own, sometimes unaware, dysfunctional lifestyle habits. Reflect on this: we frequently assume our dogs adore us unconditionally. Yet, the more I have explored this, the more evident it becomes that our bond transcends such a simplistic view. The reality is, we made the choice for them. While there are instances where profound, almost mystical connections emerge effortlessly, most bonds are gradually forged through consistent interaction and behavior. They are loyal creatures by nature and they do depend on us.

Take, for instance, a recent experience with a new colleague from the UK, who possesses a keen sensitivity to animal needs. Her encounter with my dogs left her struck by the peaceful aura that surrounds them. This harmony isn't rooted in esoteric beliefs but in a lifestyle that nurtures healthy connections and conditions. By mirroring respect, esteem, and acknowledgment of our dogs' inherent value, we lay the groundwork for a solid, trusting relationship. The reaction of my colleague to the peaceful aura of my dogs serves as a testament to the effectiveness of consistent leadership and meeting a dog's needs. This anecdote reinforces the message that our approach to building a rapport with our dogs should stem from a deeper understanding of their needs and natural behaviors. By doing so, we not only ensure their physical well-being but also foster an environment of trust, leading to a more profound and authentic bond where our dogs choose to be with us.

Establishing such healthy, balanced bonds with our dogs demands more than mere intent; it requires a lifestyle embodiment. Here, consistency is paramount. However, this doesn't imply sticking to a stringent routine—I advocate for what I term the 'no schedule schedule.' Imposing a strict daily regime contradicts their instinctual nature, fostering stress and unrest instead. Genuine consistency lies in maintaining the correct approach, not merely in repetitive actions or strict routines. Doing the same thing over and over again expecting different results, is the proverbial definition of insanity. It does more damage than benefit by eroding the dog's mental, physical, and spiritual well-being. This shows the importance of addressing all aspects of your dog's life. Achieving optimal well-being is unattainable without considering the entirety of their existence in each dimension. It's about speaking their language, adapting to their natural flow, and ensuring that you understand what your dog truly needs, and only then can you fulfill that obligation.

From Misunderstanding to Mutual Respect: The Dog-Human Dynamic

Understanding the origin of challenging behaviors in our dogs is crucial for fostering a harmonious relationship with them. These behaviors often stem from stress and unhappiness in our dogs, reflecting a misalignment between their needs and our methods of communication and interaction. This misalignment not only affects our dogs, leaving them feeling anxious and unsettled, but it also impacts our own sense of ease and confidence in our relationship with them. The key to addressing these behaviors lies in aligning our communication with the natural and instinctual language of dogs, which is through energy, body language, eye contact, subtle cues, postures, and gestures. When we begin to communicate in a manner that resonates with their instinctual understanding, we see a significant transformation. Stress-induced behaviors, rooted in anxiety and confusion, begin to dissolve, clearing the path for a more peaceful and contented existence for our dogs. This shift in communication eliminates the need for constant micro-management, correction, and control of undesirable behaviors.

At the heart of many problematic behaviors is a simple yet profound misalignment—a fundamental misunderstanding between what our dogs instinctively need and how we interact with them. This core dysfunction is the root from which all stressful and potentially dangerous behaviors spring. Recognizing and addressing this misalignment is the first step toward eliminating these behaviors, not through correction or control but through understanding and communication. By doing so, we can create an environment where our dogs feel understood and supported.

During one of my recent interactions with clients—a dedicated couple from California—perfectly illustrates the profound journey of personal and canine growth. This couple embodies the ideal client, deeply invested in their dogs and approaching their care from a spiritual and conscious perspective. They have shown remarkable progress, not just in their relationship with their dogs but in their personal development as well. Their commitment to growth through the lessons learned from their canine teachers is truly inspirational. However, their journey, like any path of true transformation, has encountered its challenges. These moments of adversity are not setbacks but opportunities for deep, impactful learning.

For instance, they noticed a sudden shift in their dog's behavior, which on the surface might seem trivial but was, in fact, a significant communication from their dog. The behavior in question was the dog placing a toy in my client's lap while she was working. Their dog was not doing this previously and when this started it alerted my clients to an inconsistency in their behavior, which was causing the dog to question them by placing the toy in her lap. They made this distinction first through awareness, and then utilizing The deep knowledge attunement technique and skill to shift this behavior immediately. While many might view this action as endearing, it reveals a deeper issue of confusion and misunderstanding about the roles and boundaries within the human-dog relationship.

This behavior, often initially met with adoration by humans, can swiftly become a source of annoyance, highlighting a fundamental miscommunication and inconsistency in the human's response. This inconsistency is characterized by a juxtaposition of irritation and engagement—where on one hand, the human may express frustration verbally or through body language, and on the other, inadvertently reinforce the behavior by interacting with the toy. This duality not only sends mixed signals to the dog but actively reinforces the behavior by associating it with attention and interaction, however negative.

While engaging with your dog in play is very important, it's crucial to stay aware. You need to ensure that this interaction and any interaction with your dog is on our terms since it reinforces that we are occupying the leadership role. It's important to note that you can't take these subtle messages lightly. When our dogs question us, our answers back to them greatly influence the trust and stability in our relationship, which affects every area of the relationship and not simply what is occurring at the moment. Dogs do not compartmentalize and if they receive information that communicates to them that they are in charge they will automatically assume they are in charge in all of their following interactions. It's like a snowball effect. Once you communicate with them that they are leading you they take that information and run with it. It isn't because they want to but because they have to. People constantly tell me that "my dogs want to be in charge" but this is not accurate whatsoever. Our dogs want us to lead the way. So while it might seem cute it's important to realize what the dog is trying to communicate because if they assume the leadership role they will experience all of the stress and discontent that comes along with it and they will act out the stress-induced behaviors, which many deem annoying or frustrating. It is important to play with your dog but it's just as important to ensure that you design it so that it aligns correctly to promote a healthy, balanced, trusting, and extraordinary bond between human and dog.

This behavior is not merely a demand for attention but a query about leadership and structure within the pack. It signifies the dog's uncertainty about who is in charge, posing an implicit question: "Am I leading, or are you?" This moment is crucial for understanding that such behaviors, while seemingly benign, are dogs' ways of expressing their need for clear guidance and leadership. The act of a dog bringing a toy to a human is multifaceted, rooted in previously reinforced behavior. It is a direct question from the dog where it is not necessarily seeking play for play's sake but is instead negotiating the terms of their relationship with their human. The human's response, particularly when they engage with the toy, may temporarily satisfy the dog, but it leaves the underlying issue of leadership and roles within their relationship unaddressed.

The mixed signals—oscillating between reprimands and engagement—essentially affirm the dog's actions, encouraging repetition rather than dissuasion. The fundamental misunderstanding lies in the human's approach to correcting the behavior without considering the dog's instinctive language and psychology. Traditional commands and reprimands, such as "get down," "no," "off," and "leave it," fall short of transforming the behavior, as they do not align with a natural and instinctive method of communication that the dog can understand and respect.

This back-and-forth of actions and reactions really shows how important it is for us to connect with our dogs in a way that makes it clear we're in charge, and we need to do it in a consistent way. It's not an argument against play or affection but a call to ensure these interactions affirm the human's position as the leader, with engagements initiated and structured on their terms. Dogs inherently seek a stable, harmonious relationship with their humans, where their roles are clearly defined, and they can feel secure and content. It is the same stability they strive for when in a pack. When dogs exhibit behaviors that challenge this dynamic, it's a call to humans to reassess how they communicate their leadership or lack thereof and provide the assurance dogs crave. This couple's experience proves the importance of consistent, clear communication with our dogs. It shows them through our actions and responses that we are capable and willing to take on the leadership role they need us to fill all while still enjoying some wonderfully rewarding and connecting play.

The revelation experienced by my client, upon observing a shift in her dog's behavior, proves the importance of mindfulness in human-dog interactions. Her story reveals a pivotal moment of awareness, recognizing that her previous responses to her dogs, although calm and affectionate, were inadvertently reinforcing an imbalance in their relationship. By becoming a conscious observer, she identified that these interactions, though seemingly benign, were validating a dynamic that placed the dogs in a leadership role, however unintentional. This insight sheds light on the complexity of human-dog relationships, emphasizing the need for consistent, aware, and stabilizing interactions. The aim is not to achieve perfection in every interaction but to foster a balanced, healthy relationship through mindful engagement. It challenges conventional perceptions of ease and natural interaction, advocating for a more deliberate approach that aligns with the dog's best interests and reinforces the desired hierarchy within the household.

Chapter 5:

Beyond Emotional Relief: Understanding Our Dogs

The Emoto Effect: Understanding the Power of Energy on Dogs

In our narrative on deepening our bond with dogs, the intriguing experiment by Masaru Emoto, a Japanese researcher known for his study on the influence of thoughts and words on the physical realm, offers an enlightening parallel. Emoto's experiment involved three containers of rice subjected to different treatments: positive affirmations, neglect, and negative energy. His findings—that the rice blessed with positive words flourished, while the rice exposed to negativity deteriorated, and the one ignored also suffered—provide a compelling illustration of the power of our interactions. This story, mirroring the essence of our journey with our dogs, emphasizes the significant impact of our words, thoughts, and the energy we bring into our relationships. The rice that thrived under positive affirmations draws a parallel to how our dogs respond to love, recognition, and respect when done properly. This is not to say that you should be smothering your dog with constant affection but that you should be interacting with them with heart coherence and heart-centered energy. This is not a physical act of love but rather the quality of presence you bring to the moment.

Conversely, the rice that turned black and moldy under the weight of negative energy reflects the harm we can do through harsh words, impatience, or misunderstanding. Our negative emotions and actions will lead to a breakdown in the trust and bond we share with our dogs, similar to the degradation observed in Emoto's experiment. The neglected rice, which also deteriorated but in its unique way, serves as a poignant reminder of the effects of indifference. In the realm of human-dog relationships, neglect doesn't always mean a lack of physical care but can also manifest as emotional disregard or inattention to their needs and communications. This can occur even with caretakers with the best of intentions. Through this analogy, we're invited to reflect on the essence of our interactions with our dogs. Emoto's work, despite its scientific critiques, underscores a universal truth applicable to our relationships with our canines: the environment we create through our thoughts, words, and actions profoundly influences their well-being and our shared harmony. This insight encourages us to cultivate a space of heart coherence, understanding, and mutual respect, ensuring a thriving, soul-nourishing bond with our dogs.

The Unseen Consequences of Dog Breeding: Beyond Aesthetics to Neurological and Behavioral Realities.

As we delve into the complex issue of breeding dogs based solely on our preferences and desires, a plethora of problems come to light. This issue is vast, and while we won't explore every facet here, it's important to touch upon the high-level problems that arise from this practice. We've become adept at altering dogs aesthetically, tailoring their appearances to suit our whims. However, the underlying issue is that while we can change their physical appearance, we inadvertently impact their neurological and behavioral health. This is particularly evident in the breeding of 'doodles' – a trend that has combined various breeds with poodles to create a myriad of new types.

Regarding Doodles, and indeed many designer breeds, it's important to be mindful of their unique neurological, behavioral, and physical complications. These dogs, often bred without considering the ramifications, are born into a world where they're predisposed to failure. I want to mention that not all doodles suffer these genetic consequences. However, in my personal experience, I have unfortunately seen a large proportion of doodles suffer from these genetic conditions. Their heightened sensitivity goes beyond the natural, instinctive sensitivity of dogs as a species. We're not merely talking about acute awareness but a susceptibility to severe anxiety issues. These breeding practices have led to the creation of dogs that are inherently timid, neurotic, and fearful. And this is just the beginning. When we consider the psychological and behavioral needs of these animals, which are often unmet by their human companions, we compound their inherent anxieties with additional stressors. Furthermore, the physical implications of such breeding practices cannot be overlooked. We're not just altering their external appearances; we're impacting their very biology, often to their detriment. A significant concern is the degradation of their gut microbiome, a crucial aspect of any living being's health. From birth, these dogs face an uphill battle, not just emotionally and mentally, but also physically.

In 'Peaceful Dog Mastery,' my goal is to illuminate these concerns, championing a philosophy that values and respects the inherent nature of dogs, as opposed to reshaping them to conform to our idealized notions. No matter what cards your dog has been dealt there is always a way to achieve greatness and to support our dogs to bring out their highest good. Whatever inherent challenges they may face, every dog is different and unique and Peaceful Dog Mastery teaches you how to support your dog for the absolute highest version of themselves no matter where they started or where they are at.

Beyond the Teddy Bear Syndrome: Addressing the Emotional Imbalance in Dog-Human Relationships.

Emoto's study is certainly intriguing, but its findings can be taken to an unhealthy extreme. Yes, absolutely you should love your dog, but unlike the rice, constant positive affirmation can be detrimental. When we shower our dogs with excessive attention and affection, we risk creating an emotional imbalance that can negatively impact their well-being. This imbalance is often rooted in a societal trend that places a disproportionate emphasis on what dogs can do for us, rather than what we can genuinely offer them in return. This oversight isn't merely a matter of routine neglect; it's a reflection of a deeper, more pervasive issue in our interactions with dogs and pretty much any other being we are relating with. The reluctance to acknowledge this is rooted in fear and discomfort. People often find it daunting to confront the notion that their interactions with their dogs might be one-sided.

For instance, intruding on a dog's personal space or engaging in constant dialogue might be comforting for a lonely individual or someone lacking emotional fulfillment, but it is stressful for the dog. This situation is not uncommon — individuals burdened with their own stress, anxiety, and emotional challenges frequently offload these onto their canine companions, treating them not as sentient beings with their own needs but rather as emotional crutches. This dynamic is like treating a dog like an emotional robot, designed solely to cater to human well-being. It's a skewed perception that fails to recognize the dog's individuality and emotional capacity.

This societal trend extends to how we breed dogs. Consider the intentional design of modern designer breeds like Doodles, crafted to mirror the comforting visage of teddy bears from our childhood. This resemblance is not serendipitous but a manifestation of our longing for emotional support from our canine teachers. It prompts us to question the fairness of projecting such expectations onto them, potentially conflicting with their authentic nature. We're shaping them to be distant from their ancestral roots, breeding them to resemble and behave like teddy bears. But what does a teddy bear represent to a child? It's a source of comfort, a security blanket that can be smothered, clung to, and cried upon. In a similar vein, we're molding dogs into living, breathing emotional anchors, expecting them to hold our emotions without considering their inherent nature. This approach to dog breeding and guardianship is a massive departure from understanding and respecting the true essence of these animals. It's an issue that 'Peaceful Dog Mastery' seeks to address — shifting the focus from what dogs can do for us to a more balanced understanding of what we owe them in terms of respect, care, and emotional space. How can we as humans give back to our dogs, repaying them for the immense inexplicable gifts they give to us?

Managing Your Own Emotional Landscape for Your Dog's Well-being

It's not uncommon to discover that caretakers are grappling with their own emotional upheavals. They share their battles with anxiety, nervousness, and a reliance on various medications such as tranquilizers, antidepressants, and anti-anxiety drugs like Xanax. Some even share their experiences with personal traumas, which, although I refrain from detailing here, very often reflect in their dog's behaviors.

The implications of this revelation are significant. In discussions about their dog's behavior in confrontational situations or leash aggression, we explore the guardian's own relationship and approach to confrontation. When I ask this, I already know the answer; they do not deal well with confrontation. The response frequently mirrors their dog's behavior, leading to a moment of realization for the dog parent—a recognition of the inadvertent projection of their unresolved traumas, previous wounding, and baggage onto their dog. This insight highlights the fact that our personal emotional challenges and struggles extend beyond ourselves, permeating the lives of our dogs. Our emotional instabilities and mental health challenges are intertwined with the wellbeing of our dogs. This understanding forms a cornerstone of this book, advocating for a holistic perspective on the human-dog relationship. It emphasizes the interconnected emotional and psychological journey we share with our dogs. Embracing this holistic view allows us to understand the importance of managing our own emotional health, not solely for our benefit but as a crucial aspect of ensuring our dogs' wellbeing.

Pandemic Puppies Discarded: The Dark Side of Emotional Dependency

The emotional dynamics between humans and dogs necessitate the acknowledgment of the significant yet often unintentional impact our human-centric views we have on our dogs. The intricate nature of this relationship has been particularly highlighted during challenging times, such as a global pandemic, shedding light on our misunderstandings and neglect of canine emotions. We project a spectrum of human emotions onto our dogs—guilt, loneliness, sadness, madness, craziness—without fully understanding the true nature of their emotional experiences. In our absence dogs wouldn't have anywhere near the behavioral challenges that they face today. If we humans are not aligned in a proper and ideal way to live closely with dogs, then the more intimately we exist with one another the more troubled the dogs become. Dogs indeed feel emotions but in a more unencumbered form compared to the complex emotional landscape of humans. Dogs are not married to their emotions like us humans are. Dogs do not attach themselves to stories of their past and do not hang on to emotional baggage. Our well-intentioned efforts to empathize can lead to misconstruing their emotional states, ascribing to them feelings they may not experience in the ways we presume.

This disconnect was starkly visible during the pandemic with the rise in the 'pandemic puppy' adoptions, symbolizing a societal trend towards seeking emotional solace in dogs amidst widespread isolation. The term 'Pandemic Puppy' became a popular label many used for dogs acquired during the pandemic, attributing their separation anxiety, lack of social skills, and stress due to the pandemic itself. In many respects, the lifestyle ushered in by the pandemic significantly supported our dogs' development. However, if individuals are initially clueless and uneducated, they are prone to blame any undesirable behaviors and traits of their dogs on external factors rather than taking responsibility and making efforts to improve. This requires thinking outside the box and committing to a more profound approach to understanding our dogs, rather than resorting to a simplistic, superficial, humanized method of raising them, which has nothing to do with their needs but everything to do with our convenience and quick fixes. Separation anxiety and other behavioral issues have existed long before the pandemic and should be addressed with accountability and dedication.

Unfortunately, the increase in adoptions was driven more by a desire to fill an emotional void in human lives rather than a deep understanding of canine needs. As the pandemic waned and normalcy began to return, many of these dogs found themselves in shelters, abandoned by those who once sought their companionship as a salve for their loneliness. This trend highlights a concerning aspect of human behavior: treating dogs as temporary emotional solutions rather than lifelong commitments. The transition back to pre-pandemic lifestyles revealed a troubling willingness to discard dogs when they no longer fit within the confines of human convenience.

Viewing dogs merely as vessels for emotional support overlooks the true depth of the dog-human bond. Dogs offer much more than emotional relief; they are capable of deep connections and loyalty. Dogs are here to be our grand master teachers. We should consider ourselves their students, as dogs have nothing to learn from us. As caretakers, our role encompasses more than seeking emotional comfort from our dogs. It's about understanding and catering to their unique emotional requirements, which are distinct from ours. Recognizing dogs as vastly intelligent beings with their own needs, we must shift our perspective away from seeing them as creatures for emotional dependence.

The emotional support dogs provide should emerge naturally from a respectful and understanding relationship, rather than being the primary basis for their role in our lives. This is an issue I see all too often, and people need to really dig deep and take a close and honest look at how they're affecting their dogs. Ensuring a dog's emotional well-being is as important as our own, necessitating careful, empathetic care. We owe it to them to consider how we can take care of our emotional states ourselves. We must approach this in a much more impactful and in charge way so that this responsibility does not fall onto them. Dogs' sensitivity to human emotions does not imply a duty to bear our emotional burdens.

Our dogs provide this exceptional catalyst for growth and heartfelt connection in us - they bring out the very best in us. And so, our goal and aspirations are ideally to stand and witness and be present to this otherworldly, magnificent embodiment that they are. It is our imperative to follow this catalyst and improve ourselves.

From Anxiety to Serenity: Dogs as Teachers of Emotional Balance

When we start to tackle our own anxieties, we stumble upon a truth that really hits home for all of us. We're pretty unique in how we let our past and our fears seep into our everyday lives, coloring our current experiences with shades of what we've been through. We often get caught up in focusing on what we're missing, instead of appreciating what we have right now, and that can lead us down a road filled with anxiety and unhappiness. The constant and cyclical repetition of what it is we don't want is taxing. We need to focus on creating a life and existence that brings us true fulfillment. This habit of letting our worries and insecurities spill over doesn't just affect us; our dogs feel it too. They're so in tune with us that they end up absorbing our emotional baggage, which can then affect their behavior and their overall happiness.

This is especially true when we talk about rescue and adoption. Sometimes, the stories we tell about our dogs, particularly those we've 'rescued' from tough situations, reveal more about us than about them. We might be drawn to dogs with the saddest stories, not just for their sake but because of the story it lets us talk about ourselves. While it might seem like we're being noble, this can sometimes mean we're putting our own needs and egos ahead of what the dog really needs. This is particularly important to me since I mainly work with rescue dogs. Canines don't dwell on their past stories of misery and neglect; they don't live their current lives based on what happened to them before. They exist in the present, not the past. Therefore, if we want to create freedom for them and for ourselves, it's crucial that we let go of those stories and focus on a new vision of the present and future, which aligns with their highest good and ours. This is yet another profound lesson our dogs are here to teach us. Living in the present moment may sound simple, but it requires deep understanding, much awareness, and significant self-work to consistently live in this elevated state. Our dogs are here to show, guide, and remind us of this path. They are here to lead the way. Are we ready to let go and step into this awakened and illuminated way of existing and living our lives?

When we cling to our dogs' past situations, constantly talking about them and feeling sorry for them, trying to overcompensate for their past experiences, we are energetically perpetuating the story and causing dysfunction in many areas of the relationship and the dog's life. This compensation, and attempts to make up for the past, place a major dampener on what we can achieve in their current blessed lives. I have seen many clients completely shift the energy and dynamics of their relationship with their dogs by consciously creating a dream-affirmative life—a vision of the future that is ideal and aligned. In many cases, that's all it takes for a long-term, powerful transformation. When humans make this shift, it organically opens the door for flowing and sustainable transformations. This is the flow state you should seek to achieve.

When we manage to self-regulate our emotions and nervous system, it has a direct effect on our dogs. Our emotional state sets the tone for our home and deeply influences our animals. So, regulating our own anxieties is not just about us; it's a shared path of healing. By taking care of our own emotional well-being, we're not just helping ourselves; we're creating a peaceful space where our dogs can flourish too. On this shared sacred journey of healing, we discover that our dogs are more than just companions; they're both our greatest mirrors and teachers, showing us the parts of our lives that need care, growth, and change. Unlike us, who might cling to old wounds and worry about future what-ifs, dogs have an incredible ability to embrace the generous present moment. They don't get bogged down by what was or what could be; they live with a deep sense of now, engaging fully with the immediate environment and the world around them. This doesn't mean dogs are untouched by what they've gone through. Certainly, shifting from one home to another, living in a stressful environment with humans, or staying in shelters can affect their feeling of security. But the heart of a dog's stress usually connects more with their present situation and whether their diverse needs are being met, rather than lingering on past or future concerns.

Thus, the essence of helping dogs overcome their challenges isn't just in recognizing their history. It's crucial to focus on making their current surroundings meet their wide-ranging needs – including behavioral, emotional, mental, environmental, nutritional, and even spiritual. Meeting these needs can significantly boost a dog's ability to recover and flourish, even after facing significant upheaval and trauma. Dogs inherently prioritize the immediate safety and well-being of themselves and their pack, embodying a profound connection to the here and now that shapes their entire existence. Dogs process trauma quite differently; their responses are largely physical, manifesting as tension or blocked energy, rather than the emotional scars and psychological issues familiar to humans. This distinction highlights their incredible resilience and capacity to move beyond past adversities, seamlessly integrating into their current environment with adaptability and presence.

Such resilience challenges our understanding of trauma in dogs, emphasizing their innate ability to rebound and thrive in the present, urging us to meet their needs comprehensively and create a supportive environment that extends beyond mere physical considerations. Witnessing dogs overcome harsh backgrounds—whether from the brutality of dog fighting or neglect—forces us to confront the resilience embedded in their nature. Dogs emerging from such trials, bearing the physical rather than emotional imprints of their past, exemplify the transformative power of adaptability and strength. This perspective shift urges us to transcend our preconceptions and appreciate the remarkable capacity of dogs to live fully in the moment, unburdened by their histories.

The significant lesson here is that we, as humans, need to align and focus all our energies in a direction that fully connects with this understanding. Supporting dogs with challenging pasts involves more than acknowledging their previous suffering. We must choose a present-focused approach; one that emphasizes consideration, thoughtful insight, and reverence. By providing a stable, nurturing environment that caters to their holistic needs, we offer dogs the opportunity to craft a new narrative, one characterized by the good that can be. This approach not only aids in their recovery but also enriches our journey with them, teaching us the value of acceptance, the power of living in the present, and the beauty of resilience.

Echoes of Emotion: Reflecting on the Complex Ties That Bind Us to Our Dogs

Watching a friend reunite with his dogs after some time apart really opened my eyes to the deep, sometimes complicated bonds we share with our canines. He playfully asked his dogs if they missed him, a question that seems simple but actually reveals a lot about how we project our feelings onto our dogs. The simple answer is no his dogs did not miss him. I don't say this to be rude, but it is the truth. Honestly, why would you want your dogs to miss you? Why would you want them to be sad and suffer while you're away? Do you want your dogs to suffer just so that you can selfishly feel loved and appreciated? This is deeply sad and contributes massively to a significant dysfunction in the way we set up our dogs. But I didn't tell him any of this. I found myself gently pointing out that his dogs probably didn't spend their time pining for him. It wasn't to belittle their connection but rather to touch on a deep human craving—the desire to be missed, to hold a special place in someone's heart, even if that someone is a dog. People are being dishonest with themselves and crafting unhappiness in their dogs so that somehow they feel special. This is one of the many reasons I ask for people to perform a deep dive inventory on all the ways in which they show up. There is a whole world of learning there for us to explore and heal.

This moment sheds light on our emotional ties and the high expectations we sometimes set for our dogs. If we're looking to our dogs to fill a void in our hearts, it might be time to take a step back and consider what's missing in our own lives. The idea of my dogs being in distress during my absence is something I find troubling; their happiness is incredibly important to me. I want my dogs to not even be phased in any way shape or form at my departure or time away. This is a true indicator of trust. Expecting them to show human-like signs of missing me adds unnecessary complexity to our otherwise smooth sailing relationship. Honestly, if you saw a human squealing, acting out of body, all over the place, screaming, jumping all over you, nipping and biting at you, urinating at the very sight of you - would you consider this behavior healthy? Would you consider this to be a peaceful, independent, trusting way of relating? I think not.

Seeing a dog's eager welcome as a sign they've been lost without us is a misunderstanding. Their enthusiastic greetings aren't about love in the human sense but rather about dependency, which can slip into an unhealthy codependency. Misinterpreting this can lead to trauma bonding, characterized not by mutual respect, love, and trust but by shared feelings of insecurity and dependence. Our dogs reflect back our emotional states, our insecurities, and our desires. We might overwhelm them without meaning to, misreading their behavior as confirmation of our own emotional stories. Lavishing them with constant affection and treats, though done with love, does not meet their true needs. Every single one of my clients who changed and shifted their energetics and ways of communicating has experienced full-on transformations in their dog and themselves. When I say every single one I mean 100% of the time and it's mostly immediately that they observe these changes.

The conversations we have with our dogs, the expectations we set, and the narratives we build around our relationship with them need to come from this higher place of understanding and connection. Asking whether our dogs missed us during our absence overlooks the point entirely; it's a question rooted in the wounded human ego rather than in understanding the heart-based existence of our dogs. To truly cultivate a flow state in our lives and in our relationships with our dogs requires stepping into a frequency of elevated consciousness, making a conscious choice every day to live from a place of deep connection, presence, and heart-centered action. This is about adopting a new way of being. It's not about the specific exercises you do at random times throughout the day, week, month, or your life with your dog. Although it might feel like a growth edge and challenge you at first, once you feel, see, experience, and understand the extraordinary gifts and transformations you are giving to your dogs, it encourages you to want to embody it—to continually, every day, step into this freedom, this optimized way of being. It is the way.

Chapter 6:

The Quest for Quick Fixes in a Device-Crazed Society

In our fast-paced world, we often seek immediate gratification, a phenomenon glaringly evident in our approach to solving problems. This tendency extends to how we address behavioral issues in dogs, where a quick fix is frequently preferred over a more thoughtful, enduring solution. Our society's fascination with gadgets and instant solutions manifests in various forms, from using shock collars and citronella sprays to silence a dog's bark, to laying down electrified mats to deter unwanted behaviors. While offering a semblance of control, these devices do not address the underlying need for education, skill development, and a shift in consciousness toward our dogs. This gadget-centric mindset parallels how some might address a persistent rash—by applying creams or taking pills for quick relief, neglecting the underlying cause, whether it be an allergy or dietary intolerance. The crux of the matter lies in understanding that superficial remedies only offer fleeting relief, and most don't even offer that. True healing, both for ourselves and our canine, begins with addressing the root causes of our discomforts and behavioral challenges. Just as eliminating certain foods from our diet can alleviate physical symptoms, so too can understanding and addressing the underlying issues behind a dog's behavior leading to genuine, lasting change.

Transformation in a dog's behavior is not the result of a quick fix but a journey—a process that demands consistency, commitment, and a deep understanding of the language and needs of our dogs. The initial improvements may seem miraculous, yet they are fragile without an ongoing commitment to awareness and a steadfast dedication to nurturing a dynamic and aligned relationship. The lure of instant solutions—be it in wealth, health, or dog "training"—is often a mirage.

Authentic and sustainable change requires patience, awareness, dedication, and an honest acknowledgment of the complexities involved. It's about embarking on a journey that fosters a deeper connection and understanding, leading to a more harmonious existence with our dogs. Just as with any aspect of life, shortcuts may seem appealing, but they seldom lead to the fulfillment or lasting results we truly desire.

Tackling the widespread issue of medicating dogs for behavioral problems unveils another significant disconnect in our society's approach to animal welfare. The startling fact that countless dogs are routinely prescribed pharmaceuticals like Prozac, Xanax, tranquilizers, and various anti-anxiety medications spotlights our collective propensity for seeking quick fixes rather than confronting the underlying causes of their distress. This route, though seemingly convenient, overlooks the fundamental needs of dogs, opting for solutions that dampen their spirits and lead to more severe behavioral issues. This reliance on medications as a go-to solution reflects our human society, where people are quick to take a pill for some sort of relief.

When clients share stories of their dogs' stress-related behaviors and medicated states, it's evident that previous strategies not only fell short but also veiled the path to true healing. We must be dedicated to forging a future where dogs are freed from unnecessary pharmaceuticals, receiving care through more natural and aligned methods. Pharmaceuticals do not solve behavior problems, they make them. Steering away from medication isn't just a preference but a mission. It's about serving as a beacon for those seeking alternatives to the pharmaceutical quick fix, advocating for practices that honor the dog's true nature and contribute to their genuine well-being. The sharp contrast between a dog managed through medication and corrective devices, and one nurtured into abundant health with holistic practices and proper support for the mind, body, and spirit could not be further apart.

This situation necessitates a profound reassessment of our relationships with dogs. It calls for dismantling the current paradigm, overly reliant on suppression and control, and constructing a new framework rooted in understanding and a deep commitment to natural, intuitive, and instinctual healing. The journey toward such transformation isn't merely about selecting different tools or techniques; it's about a fundamental change in consciousness, mindset, and energy acknowledging that our treatment of dogs reflects our values and our ability to show true discernment and comprehension. In essence, the way forward is unequivocal, necessitating a move beyond the comfort of pharmaceuticals and punitive devices towards a holistic view that sees behavioral challenges not as nuisances but as opportunities for deeper connection, learning, growth, and healing. This vision is about establishing a new norm for coexisting with and loving our dogs, ensuring their lives are enriched, fulfilling, and free from unnecessary intervention. Practically, this entails abandoning harmful devices, pharmaceuticals, and tactics that have been unjustly justified as necessary for dog training. These approaches are not just outdated; they are detrimental and abusive. The future demands a complete elimination of these practices, advocating for a coexistence based on understanding, honor, and peace, and addressing the genuine needs of our dogs.

Beyond Treats: Cultivating Trust and Respect at Every Stage of a Dog's Life.

In addressing the shortcomings of contemporary dog training methods, a critical aspect often overlooked is the overreliance on treats and the implications of such a practice. It's not the mere use of treats that's the issue — after all, as opportunistic creatures, dogs respond well to food rewards, and I certainly employ them, especially when shaping behavior in young dogs or puppies. However, the essence lies in the nuances of how, when, and why these rewards are used. A treat, in its simplicity, can be a powerful tool if employed with mindful intention and understanding. This understanding extends to the critique of positive reinforcement tactics, particularly when applied without a deep comprehension of a dog's emotional and psychological state. Attempts to comfort a stressed or anxious dog with high-pitched assurances, alongside the use of treats and a clicker, will backfire, exacerbating the dog's stress rather than alleviating it. It highlights the necessity for a more nuanced application of rewards, emphasizing the importance of timing, context, and the individual dog's needs to ensure that these tools genuinely contribute to a dog's well-being and success. We only want to employ a reward of any kind when we are encouraging and supporting a behavior we want to see exist and become the dog's new way of being, and a pathway behavior. We use rewards as a direct connection, response, and assistant so to speak in defining a new relationship with a behavior that is desired

The predominant dysfunction in dog "training" is not the treats themselves but the dependency on them. This reliance sidesteps the crucial development of a foundational bond between the dog and the human, a bond that should be deeply rooted in mutual trust and respect. The cornerstone of our approach is to emerge as 'embodied alpha leaders,' communicating in a language instinctively understood by our dogs. This is the core, the nucleus of our method, setting it apart from other philosophies in guiding and raising dogs. The analogy I often use is building a house on a shaky foundation. A house built on unstable ground will inevitably face numerous issues — constant repairs, structural weaknesses, and so forth. This is the same as the conventional approach in dog training, where an overemphasis on superficial approaches like treat-based rewards or "positive reinforcement tactics" results in an unstable, unreliable foundation in the dog-human relationship. What's more, this foundational approach to building a relationship with your dog transcends age or past experiences. Whether your dog is a brand new puppy at eight weeks old, an adolescent at five months, an adult at five years old, or even a senior at 15 years old, the opportunity to establish this solid foundation remains ever-present.

In 'Peaceful Dog Mastery,' we explore these critical aspects, guiding readers to create a lasting, meaningful, and powerful connection with their dogs, enabling them to make a profound impact on every dog they come in contact with. This knowledge is shared with friends, family, and every dog caretaker they encounter. This connection is not about temporary compliance or trick mastery; it's about forming a meaningful, respectful partnership with your canine, regardless of their age or background, lasting a lifetime. The knowledge and practices we adopt not only elevate your relationship with your dog but also catalyze substantial personal growth on your own journey. This work will completely transform and uplevel the way in which you show up in relationship to all dogs. Deeply understanding both yourself and your dogs will exponentially impact every dog you partner with for the rest of your life.

Ollie's Story: Time to Ditch Devices

The exploration into a dog's language of love can be vividly demonstrated through real-life stories, like the journey of Ollie, an Australian Labradoodle, and his guardians. This couple, novices in the realm of canine companionship, embarked on their relationship with Ollie without any predetermined beliefs, offering a fresh outlook on the bond between humans and dogs. Ollie's humans faced numerous hurdles, particularly during walks. Ollie, like many dogs, exhibited signs of stress, anxiety, and distractibility while leashed. In efforts to mitigate these behaviors, the couple explored an assortment of training tools, from prong collars to gentle leaders. They watched countless YouTube videos and opinions of "trainers" who did nothing but steer them down a path of confusion and disharmony. This situation reflects the common problem: the reliance on physical tools and contraptions, including torture devices, and spray bottles, as well as the misuse of treats as quick fixes for more complex behavioral challenges. In essence, focusing on everything except what is real for the dog.

Hearing the word torture devices might make you take a step back and say "I don't use torture devices on my dog" but there are people out there using devices that directly hurt their dog and its most sensitive areas like its nose or genitals. Any and all of these devices torture a dog's spirit. Would you want a tight strap over the most sensitive parts of your body, or frankly, around any part of your body? Would you want tight metal daggers piercing your skin every time you tried to perform a job description you were given? Would you be comfortable with a thick, heavy electronic device shackled to your neck, causing pain and discomfort every time you reacted in stress to the task you were given? Would you ever use a shock collar on your child? I hope your answer is no. The stark contrast between how we treat our dogs versus our children brings to light a fundamental inconsistency in our understanding of care and love. Relying on mechanisms like shock collars, even if deemed as 'just a beep,' reveals a profound disconnect in our approach to addressing behavioral issues. If such measures are unthinkable for children, why do they become acceptable for our dogs, often considered as family members? How can we call our dogs our children and say that we love them so much all while using detrimental devices and shocking them? That is not love; we need to trust and know that there is a better way.

A turning point for Ollie and his guardians was the decision to alter their strategy, moving from a reliance on physical restraints to one grounded in a deep understanding, empowerment, and comprehension. By embodying the qualities of a true embodied Alpha leader, defined by consistency, directness, and presence rather than disconnection, dominance, or even positive reinforcement; they cultivated a more meaningful bond with Ollie. None of these devices, collars, gadgets, gimmicks, or training tools would ever be needed when we understand the nature of our dogs. By becoming fluent in their language and embodying the alpha leadership role, these become unnecessary. With this understanding as our bedrock and foundation, there's no need to resort to external tools beyond the powerful connection we share with our dogs. First, we must remember and relearn these most important facets, which will pave the way for the freedom we are deeply searching for.

This shift entailed abandoning the array of training tools in favor of a basic flat collar and leash. Basic, pure, and simple is always the right way. Put simply, less is more. The impact was significant: Ollie not only became more responsive and attuned but also visibly more content, balanced, and self-assured. The relationship that evolved with his pack was built on mutual trust and understanding, a notable departure from their earlier struggles. Ollie's story accentuates a crucial lesson in canine companionship: the significance of recognizing and honoring a dog's authentic character and requirements. It challenges the conventional view that "training" necessitates physical coercion, promoting a more connected and comprehensive approach instead. By understanding and respecting Ollie's language, his guardians learned to communicate in a way that acknowledged his limits and celebrated his true self, leading to a remarkable transformation in their relationship.

Chapter 7:

Whole Dog Wellness: A Three-Pronged Approach to Dog Care - Environment, Nutrition, Veterinary Practices

The Holistic Habitat: Managing Your Dog's Environment

Our choices, from the food we offer to the products we utilize in our homes, have a massive impact on our dogs' health and well-being. I pay meticulous attention to every detail of my dogs' surroundings, including the materials of their eating and drinking vessels, the materials of their sleeping areas, and the cleaning products used in our shared environment. This level of care extends to the vehicles they travel in and the outdoor spaces where they play. Grasping the influence of a dog's surroundings on their well-being goes beyond acknowledging mere physical comforts; it requires a deep understanding of their holistic needs. Every aspect of a dog's surroundings, from the air they breathe to the ground they walk on, plays a part in their enriching daily experiences.

When contemplating a dog's living conditions, the mind often drifts to visible elements such as cozy beds or colorful toys. Yet, the essence of a conducive environment extends far beyond these items. It's about creating a space that satisfies their fundamental needs, rather than conforming to our human notions of luxury. For example, a lavish dog bed might seem appealing, but dogs genuinely flourish in settings that embrace natural, sustainable, and organic materials. Each element of their habitat, from the furnishings to the bedding, should ideally be derived from organic, eco-friendly sources, or crafted from recycled, non-toxic substances. The sensitivity of dogs, particularly through their absorbent paw pads and their noses, exposes them to the myriad of toxins present on surfaces cleaned with harsh chemicals. This risk is exacerbated as dogs instinctively groom themselves, inadvertently ingesting harmful substances. This scenario highlights the imperative for dog caretakers to exercise discernment in their choice of cleaning agents and all household products prioritizing those that are safe and devoid of toxic ingredients.

Each decision, from the water they drink to the toys they engage with, is made with their health, vitality, longevity, and happiness in mind. I want to emphasize that this isn't about being perfect. You don't need to become obsessive or neurotic about every little detail. It's about being aware of what contributes to disease and complications in the well-being of both animals and humans, as well as what fosters optimal health, vitality, and abundance. Paying close attention to and enhancing their physical surroundings are essential steps in fostering their overall mental well-being and guiding positive behavioral health outcomes. This deliberate approach not only addresses their immediate needs but also supports a foundation for long-term stability and vibrant homeostasis. The physical bond we share with our dogs goes beyond merely safeguarding them against the toxins and pollutants that pervade our world. It's about recognizing that these external factors have a deep impact on their mental, behavioral, and physical states. The significance of the home environment for dogs goes beyond just the physical space; it encompasses how we interact with them and meet their true needs.

Consider a child labeled with ADHD who consumes foods filled with preservatives, artificial ingredients, and sugar; expecting them to remain focused and grounded can be unrealistic. Similarly, in the canine realm, behaviors often labeled as reactive, nervous, anxious, or even 'aggressive' warrant a deeper investigation beyond initial appearances. Such behaviors typically arise from underlying stress, manifesting in various forms from withdrawal to overt reactivity. It's vital to examine the multitude of factors contributing to these behaviors. In my experience with dogs labeled as aggressive, it's apparent that this label is often misused, not truly reflecting the dog's true nature. This misunderstanding usually arises from not fully grasping the root causes of their actions. The human's involvement and dedication are crucial to achieve a real transformation. If a dog's diet remains filled with inappropriate, inflammatory substances, expecting a behavioral overhaul is unrealistic. This scenario calls for a reassessment of our approach, taking into account every factor affecting our dogs' behavior, including their diet, the products surrounding them, and our interactions with them. These elements collectively play a role in either amplifying or reducing their stress levels.

Addressing the often-overlooked importance of diet in a dog's overall well-being is essential. This isn't a selective strategy but a core principle for all dogs I work with. The significant impact of a dog's diet on their behavior and health is frequently underestimated, even by the health-conscious who might not extend their dietary principles to their dogs. Through my experience, I've observed the most remarkable and profound changes in a dog's behavior and overall demeanor, brought about simply by overhauling every product the dog consumes on a daily basis. It's a powerful and crucial shift, underscoring the transformative potential of diet. This transformation relies heavily on the human's readiness to implement necessary dietary changes. It's a collaborative effort, where each aspect critically influences the dog's path to transformation.

Why Quality Trumps Quantity for Your Dog's Exercise

In the sphere of canine wellness, striking a balance in physical activity is crucial. The prevailing myth that dogs need relentless, intense exercise or daily participation in daycare is not only misguided but could be very detrimental. On one side, we observe dogs living sedentary lifestyles, confined indoors with scant stimulation, which can impair both their physical and mental health. On the flip side, some dogs are pushed into excessive physical exertion, not to meet their genuine exercise needs but rather as an ill-conceived strategy to address hyperactivity or behavioral issues. This can lead to overexertion and stress, offering no advantage to the dog's overall wellness; it actually makes them more stimulated and agitated. Dogs sleep an average of 18-22 hours per day - they reserve their energy for survival.

Understanding that canine well-being hinges not on the quantity but the quality of movement and energy release is pivotal. Physical activities should be aligned with a dog's innate instincts and needs, fostering a balance that honors their physical and mental capacities. Integrating a harmonious mix of activities, and encouraging natural play and exploration, can make a significant difference. Dogs with a balanced exercise regimen return home not only at peace but also noticeably invigorated, in huge contrast to the overt weariness often seen after exposure to toxic, stressful, overstimulating experiences. This balanced approach to exercise also acknowledges that excessive physical activity is not a panacea for behavioral challenges. Often, such issues stem from unmet psychological needs or environmental factors rather than mere physical inactivity. Hence, a comprehensive strategy that encompasses thoughtful exercise, body movement, mental engagement, and a supportive environment is paramount.

The ethos of Conscious Dog Education in relation to a dog's physical activity transcends traditional practices. It's about discerning and honoring the dog's inherent rhythms and needs. Emphasizing quality movement and energy release, tailored to each dog's unique instincts and physical capabilities, is at the heart of this philosophy. Aligning exercise routines with a dog's instinctual preferences cultivates a setting conducive to their growth. This method not only ensures physical fitness but also nurtures mental and emotional well-being, reflecting a deep respect for their essence and a dedication to their comprehensive health. This approach strengthens the unique bond between humans and their canine teachers.

Mastering the Art of Quality Social Interaction

How dogs get along with others around them is really important for their happiness. Dogs, by nature, are highly social beings, yet their social requirements are optimally fulfilled within the confines of their familiar group, rather than through interactions with a multitude of unknown dogs, as often encountered in dog parks or daycare settings. Such environments, teeming with unfamiliar faces, can be overwhelming and inadvertently foster stress and unwelcome behaviors. This environment completely goes against their hardwired nature and species code; it is totally alien for them to be thrust into a situation like this. Many of you might be taken aback by this. There are so many people who take their dog to the dog park to the beach or other social settings.

There is a way to design these experiences to make them as stress-free as possible, empowering the dog parent on how to navigate these situations and set their dogs up for success. For example, if someone is planning to enter a dog area where there are multiple dogs interacting and the person or dog doesn't know them, I always advise my clients to use their intuition. You don't just rush into situations like that without testing the waters and feeling the energy—not in a nervous or hesitant way, but in the way an alpha would, with thoughtful consideration. We all know that we can catch the vibe. If the energy is chaotic, with lots of barking and dogs teaming up on each other, and the humans are running around trying to correct their dogs' behavior desperately, this is not the ideal situation to walk into. It's best to avoid it and come back when the conditions are calmer, there are fewer dogs, and the dogs present have a settled, flowing energy. As the embodied alpha leader, it is always your job not only to protect your dog but to create situations where it's very easy for them to do well and succeed and very hard for them not to. Custom Tailoring social encounters is therefore essential. Organizing intimate gatherings or one-on-one play sessions with trusted canine and human companions can markedly enrich your dog's social experiences. This approach to selective socialization honors their inherent social tendencies while safeguarding against undue stress, ensuring interactions are both enjoyable and beneficial.

Vitality and Vigor: The Role of Diet in Enhancing Dog Longevity

Diving deep into canine nutrition is a pivotal aspect of Conscious Dog Education. It's unfortunately something that has been made both overcomplicated and overwhelming. I'd like to emphasize the critical influence of dietary choices on our dogs' health and longevity. This journey begins the moment we welcome a puppy into our lives, underscoring the importance of a diet that not only satisfies their taste buds but also nourishes their body in accordance with their biological needs. By providing a species-appropriate and healthy diet, we truly meet our dogs' nutritional needs.

Despite dogs consuming products that do not positively contribute to their health and well-being, it's important to recognize that this is often because they are opportunistic feeders. Mass dog food companies exploit this by adding sugar, toxic additives, and palatability enhancers that stimulate a dog's desire for more. This probably sounds familiar. Similar things are done in the human food industry because quite frankly they are not actually concerned for your health; they are purely profit-driven. This approach not only undermines the genuine nutritional needs of our dogs but also adversely affects their health in every way. The challenge often lies in deciphering the myriad of options the market presents, many of which are cloaked in attractive packaging and persuasive advertising, yet may fall short in nutritional integrity.

As conscientious caretakers, it's our duty to peer beyond these facades, selecting real foods that genuinely contribute to our dogs' vitality. At the heart of Conscious Dog Education is a holistic perspective on nutrition, advocating for a thorough evaluation of every facet of a dog's diet and environmental exposures. This ethos transcends fleeting dietary fads and the allure of premium price tags, grounding itself in a well-informed, biologically attuned approach to nourishing our dogs. In our quest for canine wellness, it's incumbent upon us to challenge conventional dogma, scrutinize the motives of the "pet" food industry, and make informed choices that truly enhance our dogs' quality of life. This commitment to their well-being is not just about extending their years but enriching the quality of each moment they share with us.

The Detriment of Dry: Unveiling Kibble's Impact on Canine Health

As we explore deeper into the nuances of canine nutrition, I need to address the production of dry kibble. Dry kibble is one of the most pervasive issues in canine nutrition. It starts with using unhealthy ingredients that are void of any nutrients. Then it goes through a high-heat process that fundamentally alters the nutritional profile of the ingredients, resulting in a product that lacks the vital nutrients essential for our dogs' health. To speak candidly, the heating process essentially turns it into carcinogenic cardboard. This systemic issue extends beyond mere nutrient depletion; it reflects a broader concern about the overall health implications of feeding our dogs a diet that does not align with their physiological needs.

The parallels between human dietary habits and the choices we make for dogs are striking. Just as processed foods detrimentally affect human health, a similar pattern is evident in dogs, with poor dietary choices contributing to a range of health issues, including the troubling rise in canine diabetes and all different forms of cancer. Yes, canine diabetes. The manifestations of an inappropriate diet – such as foul odors, obesity, a lackluster coat, digestive disturbances, allergies, chronic infections, and many more – are indicative of a deeper dietary misalignment, underscoring the need for a shift towards more biologically species-appropriate, nutrient-rich feeding practices. The key takeaway here is that dogs with access to real, alive food—even if it's just human leftovers—are significantly better off than those on a diet made up entirely of dry, dead rations.

It's vital to highlight that dry food is essentially dead food only designed to keep the dog alive. Remarkably, the oldest living dogs across the globe have been found to subsist solely on human food, never having consumed a speck of commercial "dog food" in their lives, proving the detrimental impact of dry dog food as a silent and eventually overt killer. It's also crucial to address a widespread misunderstanding regarding wet food—many people mistakenly believe it to be healthier than dry kibble, when in fact, it is equally processed and equally toxic. This insight is essential in reevaluating the dietary choices we make for our dogs.

The argument for a biologically appropriate diet is compelling. Dogs flourish on a regimen that emulates their natural consumption patterns, encompassing fresh, whole foods that are minimally processed, nutrient-dense, and devoid of detrimental additives. Such a diet not only acts as a deterrent to various diseases but also significantly enhances the dog's overall quality of life. The positive outcomes are evident — from a vibrant coat and fresher breath to diminished body odor and a marked increase in energy, vitality, and well-being. Embracing a more supportive and nourishing diet for our canines represents not just a fleeting fad but a fundamental return to the essentials of canine biology. It challenges us to reassess our feeding choices, putting the health and well-being of our dogs above the lure of convenience offered by products like dry kibble. Despite its appeal, the ease of kibble feeding is outweighed by the comprehensive health advantages afforded by a diet that respects the physiological needs of dogs. The acceptance of substandard food, which would be deemed unacceptable or even illegal in other countries, must end. Our dogs deserve the same quality and care in their diet as we aspire for ourselves.

As guardians, we bear the onus of making enlightened decisions regarding dogs' nutrition. This commitment transcends mere surface-level considerations, urging us to go the extra mile concerning dogs' nutritional needs and to make choices that holistically nurture their health. This takes time, thoughtful research, and an understanding of how to read between the lines and know exactly what is in our dog's food. It is important not to be tricked into believing clever packaging and buzz words, which the industry does with expertise in convincing consumers to purchase their products. We must become advocates for our dog's health. Since traditional Western vets are part of a profit-driven industry, where the more sick dogs that come through their doors the more money they make; it's important to take what they say with a grain of salt. By adopting this thoughtful approach to nutrition, we elevate our role from mere caregivers to advocates for our dogs' health and vitality. This is the crux of Conscious Dog Education — a path that deepens our bond with our dogs, founded on mutual respect and a shared dedication to their optimal well-being. It's a journey that not only enriches their lives but also enhances the fulfillment and joy we derive from our relationship with them. This expands beyond supporting mother nature and the environment alone, it creates a ripple effect of high frequency and harmonization.

Hunting to Nurturing: Reimagining Dog Diets

Since dogs are opportunistic feeders, which is ingrained in their genetic code, there is no way to alter their intrinsic feeding behaviors, which are both primal and instinctual. Our contemporary feeding practices often diverge from these natural tendencies, not only by introducing potentially harmful substances into their diets but also by diminishing the inherent ritualistic aspect of their eating habits. Witnessing a wild wolf pack's coordinated hunt and communal meal-sharing is a stark reminder of this intricate and communal sustenance approach, a facet often missing in our domesticated dogs' lives. In our role as caretakers, we symbolically step into the shoes of an Alpha, guiding and nurturing these magnificent creatures. Our duties surpass the simple act of providing nourishment; they extend to fostering their primal needs. This includes presenting resources and experiences that resonate with their instinctual drives and contribute to their holistic well-being.

The practice of 'free feeding,' where food is made available all day or is left out for periods of time fully accessible, contradicts the dog's innate understanding of food as a scarce and valuable resource. This concept holds true across breeds, from Bichon Frisé to Labradors to street dogs and village dogs, who all possess an inherent recognition of the natural rarity and worth of sustenance. Leaving food out and accessible for our dogs is destructive not only for their psychological state but also for their physical state. In the wild, the hunt is a deliberate and strategic affair, demanding teamwork, intellect, and skill. This transcends mere consumption, engaging their cognitive abilities, challenging their instincts, and fulfilling their evolutionary roles. As conscientious guardians, our aim should mirror these natural behaviors, incorporating elements of this ancestral ritual into their daily lives. Such an approach not only addresses their nutritional needs but also stimulates their minds, honoring their primal instincts and enabling them to flourish in a domesticated world. Assuming the mantle of a thoughtful caretaker transcends basic feeding; it involves celebrating their lineage, acknowledging their intrinsic nature, and enhancing their life experiences. This philosophy, anchored in deep understanding and respect, is the bedrock of our approach to optimizing canine nourishment and care, fostering a deep and harmonious connection with our canine companions.

Breaking the Clock: Rethinking Dog Feeding Schedules

The practice of adhering to strict feeding schedules is a topic that warrants a closer examination. This widely accepted routine is based on a misunderstanding of canine psychology, suggesting that dogs thrive on consistent, unchanging feeding times—a notion that contradicts their inherent nature. Unlike humans, dogs do not perceive their day in segments designated for specific activities, as they lack a concept of time as we understand it. Dogs are remarkably adept at forming associations, a skill that allows them to predict events based on environmental cues and the routines of their human companions. They don't rely on clocks to anticipate their next meal but rather on the sequence of daily events—the morning hustle, the sound of the kitchen light, the cabinet being opened—which they link to feeding time. While this predictive behavior may seem advantageous, it actually goes against their instinctual grain.

The routine of feeding at precise times each day removes the element of unpredictability inherent to a dog's natural lifestyle, where meals in the wild are neither guaranteed nor regularly timed. This lack of predictability is essential for stimulating their mental and emotional well-being, keeping them mentally invigorated and engaged. While it may seem that your dog, living far from its wild ancestors' lifestyle, doesn't adhere to the same rules, it's crucial to remember that their psychological makeup remains unchanged. Food isn't guaranteed, and the process of feeding is ritualistic, involving many layers and components where the pack operates together as a well-oiled machine. This unity, working in grace and resembling poetry in motion, is all for the survival of the pack. We cannot minimize the significance of these behaviors. Understanding that the psychology and innate behaviors surrounding food and feeding rituals are deeply ingrained, we see that these aspects are not just about survival but are a complex interplay of behaviors that reinforce social bonds and hierarchy within the pack.

This issue extends beyond mere nutrition, highlighting a deeper misunderstanding of how we provide care for our dogs. By imposing human-centric routines, we may inadvertently neglect their need to engage in natural pack behaviors. Dogs instinctively look for leadership and structure from their pack leaders—a role that humans can assume as their guardians. Failure to acknowledge and cater to their psychological needs can result in placing them in unnatural roles, affecting dogs of all breeds, ages, sexes, and backgrounds. Addressing this challenge calls for a significant shift in our approach to canine care, necessitating a holistic understanding of their psychological and instinctual needs. This involves rethinking not only our feeding practices but also our daily interactions with them, ensuring we fulfill our roles as guardians.

Exploring the role of an Alpha leader in the dog-human dynamic reveals a complex interplay of responsibilities, including initiating, providing, protecting, and managing the pack in a manner that is coherent, grounded, and aligned. A key aspect of this leadership role involves how we structure routines and environments, in all aspects of life. Establishing a predictable routine, particularly around meal times, but really all of the time, can inadvertently place dogs in a perceived leadership position, especially if food is left accessible at all times or provided on a rigid schedule. This can signal to the dog that they have the autonomy to decide when to eat, potentially undermining our position as the pack leader and leading to various behavioral issues. These approaches are extreme and neither one supports the ideal life for our dogs. When people use these methods the relationship and the way we set our dogs up is not balanced and not in an ideal flow state.

A dog that perceives itself as the leader (or most likely completely confused as to who is) in one aspect, such as feeding, may exhibit problematic behaviors in other areas, including resource guarding, coveting, or demanding attention. These behaviors are not just minor inconveniences but indicative of a deeper struggle for leadership within the household. This philosophy not only pertains to how we feed our dogs but also reflects a broader societal stance on nutrition and environmental stewardship. The choices we make in nourishing our dogs mirror our values and practices in nourishing ourselves and caring for our environment. This comprehensive discussion on nutrition and care for our dogs invites further exploration into aligning our practices with the principles of conscious dog education and holistic health, emphasizing the interconnectedness of our decisions and their impact on the well-being of our canine teachers and ourselves.

Bridging the Gap: Human Health Awareness vs. Canine Nutritional Neglect

It's surprising how health-conscious individuals who are diligent about their and their family's diets often neglect to consider their dogs' nutritional needs. This gap is perplexing and disheartening, as they express a deep love for their dogs and a desire for their long-term health but overlook how their feeding practices are detrimental. Once awareness is brought to this blind spot, the rewards are beyond incredible. Making this connection and distinction leads to transformative changes, where everyone, including their beloved dogs, starts living the most uplifted, vibrantly healthy existence. This heightened level of well-being for all involved is not just beneficial—it's deeply fulfilling and a testament to the power of informed compassionate care.

The repercussions of such oversight are substantial. Dogs should be living into their 30s. Back in the 1970s, the lifespan of breeds like Golden Retrievers was around 17-20 years old. This has significantly decreased over the decades to now only 9-12 years old. This isn't due to natural causes, but rather the cumulative effects of a processed, toxin-rich diet, along with the many ways in which we are unknowingly or unconsciously poisoning our dogs. This pattern of seemingly healthy dogs developing aggressive cancers in mid-life points directly to the toxic burden they've endured.

Our pets are exposed to some of the most toxic conditions imaginable due to our choices. The shift towards cheaper, more convenient dog food options plus the detrimental household chemicals, "preventative" medications, and over vaccination just to name a few has resulted in a diet and environment that contributes to a slow deterioration of their health. Far from the vibrant long and healthy life that is free of disease, skin conditions, gut health issues, diabetes, autoimmune disorders, etc. Dogs, as opportunistic feeders, have no choice in what they eat. A dog will never intentionally starve itself, so most dogs will continue to consume biologically inappropriate rations, which cause low to mid-level markers of inflammation until the body can no longer cope and succumbs to the toxic load placed upon it.

I'd like to point out a real-life situation to highlight an important disconnection. I recall a memorable experience with a client who was the President of the University of Chicago. The client cared for three Inuit dogs, magnificent animals. Despite having the resources to provide the best for these dogs, their diet was suboptimal, leading to persistent health problems. It became evident that a change was necessary. Introducing the concept of a dietary and environmental overhaul was initially met with hesitation. But a breakthrough occurred when I noticed something in her email signature. There was a strongly worded quote "Factory farming is illegitimate and evil don't enable it." This was clearly a cause my client was extremely passionate about. The major ingredient or protein source in her dogs' food was factory-farmed sick and diseased animals; not animals that are raised, fed, housed, and slaughtered with honor and respect. I pointed this out to her and her unintentional hypocrisy clicked in her mind. This realization helped her see that the values she advocated for in one aspect of her life were being neglected in the care of her dogs. It also served as a major revelation and aha moment as a whole. Prompted by this insight, she took my hand and we approached her computer, and together we began exploring healthier dietary options for her dogs. This moment served as a revelation for both of us, emphasizing that caring for our dogs is intricately linked to our broader life values, especially those concerning environmental stewardship. This incident proves that dog care transcends basic responsibilities. It's about ensuring our actions and choices, particularly regarding our environment, align with our values, fostering a setting where our dogs can flourish in harmony with nature. This principle holds true for all individuals, regardless of their societal or professional standing.

Addressing canine behavioral issues often leads to quick fixes such as professional "training" or medications like tranquilizers such as Trazadone or a canine version of Prozac and Xanax. This approach reflects a broader societal tendency to overlook underlying problems in favor of immediate solutions as discussed in the previous chapter. True support for our dogs involves a comprehensive understanding of their needs, The way they think, and how they experience life- extending beyond behavior to encompass their overall well-being. In dealing with various clients, I've noticed how certain lifestyle choices inadvertently compromise canine health even beyond diet. The use of harmful household chemicals, toxic candles, air fresheners, fragrance plug-ins for the home and vehicle, and unsafe dog toys and accessories introduces unnecessary risks to our dogs' well-being. Such decisions, often made without full awareness, can have significant negative impacts on our dogs' health.

Beyond the Clinic: Unpacking the Commerce-Driven Veterinary Practice

The veterinary industry, while indispensable, veers towards a commercial orientation that may not always align with optimal wellness. My encounters with traditional veterinary practices have been revealing, shedding light on how profit-driven motives can sometimes eclipse the foundational goal of abundant animal health and longevity. This was starkly highlighted during an interaction with a vet who, quite candidly, identified more as a businessman than a healer. This unfortunately is a very common occurrence. Such admissions, though rare, peel back the curtain on a concerning trend where the financial bottom line can sometimes override the best interest of our canine best friends. I've been working closely with vets for over 25 years and I don't make these statements flippantly. These experiences over the years have shown me that this is the issue with the entirety of the traditional Western veterinary world.

The topic of vaccinations further illustrates this dilemma. The prevailing 'more is better' mindset can lead to an excessive chemical burden on our dogs, potentially undermining their immune resilience. Certain vaccines, like the one for Lyme's disease, may pose more risk to a dog's cellular integrity than the disease itself, raising questions about the balance between prevention and the potential for long-term health ramifications. The issue of over-vaccination is just one piece of a larger puzzle. The specters of cancer and canine diabetes loom as stark reminders of the consequences of a lifetime marred by inadequate nutrition and unnecessary medical interventions. This realization that the business of Westernized approaches to veterinary care thrives not on the health but rather on the ailments of dogs can be unsettling. Yet, embracing this truth is a crucial step towards advocating for a more enlightened approach to canine health care, one that prioritizes genuine well-being over routine interventions. I'm not arguing that vets are evil or that they don't provide care for dogs; I just want people to realize that they don't always have your dog's best interest at the forefront of their minds.

Chapter 8:

The Spiritual Nature of Dogs

There is a profound spiritual connection between humans and dogs, a bond deeply rooted in history and spanning various cultures across the globe. In regions like Tibet, dogs are not merely companions but revered spiritual entities, celebrated through festivals that show their sacred significance. In short, they really do treat dogs as Gods. This spiritual connection with dogs transcends the traditional human understanding of emotions, offering a unique, intuitive bond that extends beyond the physical and emotional realms and into the spiritual realm. Despite the universal nature of this spiritual bond, cultural disparities in the treatment of dogs highlight a broader commentary on human spiritual progression or regression. Overall, I'd unfortunately say that we are regressing and I hope that this book can work to shift this paradigm. The reverence seen in some cultures starkly contrasts with the harsh realities in others, where dogs face extreme cruelty, illustrating a significant disconnect from the spiritual essence dogs embody. For example, in South Korea, dogs are not treated with any respect at all. Their treatment is so uncompassionate that it resembles how farm animals are viewed, extending even to instances where dogs are tortured and then consumed. I hope that over time these practices can change and that people across all countries and cultures can understand that dogs are not put on this earth for our abuse, but as profound spiritual teachers for us to learn from.

The often-overlooked recognition of the spiritual dimension dogs bring to our lives points to a deeper disconnection from an instinctual understanding. Put plainly, many people don't realize how much dogs contribute to our spiritual well-being. Not recognizing this sacred bond shows that we're losing touch with our natural instincts and deeper, more ethereal understanding of life. Dogs, in their simplicity and purity, embody a spirit untainted by human complexities, offering us insights into a spirituality that is immediate and genuine. In understanding this bond, it's crucial to view our relationship with dogs beyond our emotional projections, appreciating their intrinsic divine presence. This presence is palpable. Even individuals who consider themselves atheists, who don't believe in God, still have this kind of otherworldly affinity for their dogs. There is this higher vibration and connectivity that regardless of personal religious views people still feel and understand even if they are not conscious of it. It's a metaphysical experience to be around dogs.

In the revered traditions of Native American and Shamanic healing circles, there exists a profound reverence for the unique vibration and energy emitted by medicine dogs. These creatures are not merely animals; they are embodiments of healing properties whose presence elevates the spiritual experience. Their absence is deeply felt, leaving a real void that proves our mortal limitations. In these cultures, they understand that we are just mere mortals among these awe-inspiring creatures. Engaging with a dog brings us into contact with an ineffable frequency, a vibrational energy that, though elusive to our conscious understanding, irresistibly draws us closer. It's this connection that taps into the universal oneness, the very essence of the source, creating a bridge between the earthly and the divine. Historically, it was humans that initiated the bond with wolves. They helped guide us towards a higher consciousness, not through dominance, but through mutual recognition of the qualities each brought to the partnership. This alliance allowed humans to access a deeper level of awareness, with dogs playing pivotal roles in various spiritual practices, acting as guides and teachers, enhancing healing and spiritual experiences.

The spiritual essence of dogs resonates as a unique frequency, a connection that surpasses traditional human emotions like love, tapping into something more primal and universal. The connection shared with dogs is invaluable and deeply meaningful, extending beyond the conventional notion of dogs as mere embodiments of pure love. My perspective on their interactions, both amongst themselves and with humans, ventures beyond traditional definitions of love, seeking a more nuanced understanding. In relationships with dogs, trust is paramount, forming the foundation for a deeper, more meaningful bond. It's no surprise that most people value their relationship with their dogs over a lot of if not all of their relationships with humans. This is why across the globe over 57% of households have dogs. Imagine walking through a vast art gallery filled with abstract and modern art pieces. Visitors may pass by countless canvases without a second thought, their emotions untouched by the swirling colors and bold shapes. Yet, when they come upon a single painting of a vulnerable dog, their hearts are stirred, and empathy floods in, illustrating how our compassion can be selective and profound for the innocence of animals compared to our response to human tribulations. There is something in the very essence of dogs that we are drawn to. However, observing human-dog interactions reveals a frequent lack of trust, often due to inadequate leadership and understanding from humans. This lack of trust, evident in the behavior of both dogs and their caretakers, proves the need for a deeper comprehension and a shift in human approach. Considering dogs as 'divine channels' illuminates their significant spiritual role in our lives, irrespective of individual beliefs. Their presence has the power to transform skepticism into faith, embodying the essence of spirituality in the most pristine form. They stand as living symbols of all that is pure and genuine, like sacred icons and exemplars of these qualities.

The notion that we might have shared past lifetimes with our dogs is fascinating, evidenced by the intense, almost inexplicable understanding between a dog and its human. This connection, seemingly eternal, suggests a pre-existing bond, an unspoken understanding that transcends mere familiarity. It's hard to put into words but there is an energy or a feeling that is so strong that it seems impossible that their interactions in this life are enough to justify it. This spiritual linkage underscores the necessity for humans to evolve, as our interactions with dogs often reveal our limitations and the need to elevate our consciousness to resonate with their purity and presence. Dogs exemplify living in the generous present moment, free from the burdens of past experiences or future worries. They offer a lesson in true mindfulness and presence that many humans find challenging to embody let alone even consider or think about. This chapter aims to highlight the sacred essence of our bond with dogs, urging us to move beyond narrow viewpoints and welcome the profound spiritual connection they bring into our lives. It's a connection that enriches our existence, expanding our insight into our own being, the natural world, and the universe at large. Crucially, it's noted that individuals from diverse backgrounds who share their lives with dogs experience this ineffable spiritual bond. This universal feeling, though hard to articulate, profoundly impacts our understanding of spirituality and interconnectedness.

Chapter 9:

The Human Aspect: Our Responsibility to Our Dogs

The Accountability Factor

Reflecting on a recent interaction with one of my clients highlights the pivotal role of human commitment in the human-dog relationship. This client, whose dog had previously undergone an intensive educational program with me that achieved significant improvements, expressed dissatisfaction with her dog's behavior a year later. Despite the dog's stellar progress post-program, the lingering issues underscored a crucial aspect: the human element. The client's message was a mix of discontent and acknowledgment of the effectiveness of the techniques provided. Yet, it revealed a stark disconnect—while praising the methods, she lamented her dog's reactivity, overlooking her lack of follow-through with the program. This scenario is emblematic of a broader issue where clients seek solutions without fully committing to the necessary changes in their behavior and approach. A dog is not an appliance that can be sent away and "fixed" for life. It's our job to step in and maintain our side of the relationship.

Each session with this client was an opportunity for reflection and adjustment, yet it became clear that the guidance wasn't being implemented. The presence of her boyfriend, showing visible frustration, further showed the gap between knowledge and action. This dissonance between understanding what works and the willingness to apply it consistently was at the heart of the issue. The message she sent was a clear illustration of this gap—a blend of dissatisfaction with her dog's behavior and an acknowledgment of the effectiveness of the teachings. It highlighted a significant blind spot: a failure to take responsibility for her role in her dog's behavior and well-being. This lack of accountability, the inability to recognize one's impact on the dog's experience, is a common hurdle in achieving lasting change.

Dogs, in their essence, mirror the energy, intentions, and consistency of their human counterparts. They thrive on clarity, stability, and leadership. When these are lacking, due to our complexities and layers of personal issues, it directly affects our dogs, burdening them with a "job description" they are ill-equipped to fulfill. This woman's situation, where her dog behaved differently in her care versus a more supportive and committed environment, illustrates the impact of human behavior and Embodied Alpha energy on our dogs. This narrative serves as a potent reminder of the need for caretakers to introspect, align their actions with their goals for their dogs, and commit genuinely to the process. It's about more than just learning techniques; it's about embodying them and becoming a consistent and confident presence for our dogs. Recognizing this is the first step towards fostering a harmonious and fulfilling human-dog relationship.

In my practice, witnessing the behavioral transformation in dogs often highlights not just their adaptability but also the guardians' shifts in mindset and approach. It's on us humans to evolve personally into better people for our dogs and for ourselves. Through enlightened dog education, we learn to see our dogs not as servants but as life partners, each with their own individuality, needs, and communication styles. Recognizing that so-called 'problematic' behaviors often signal deeper issues invites us to reevaluate our understanding of their true intrinsic nature and needs.

One of the key tenets of conscious dog education is to dive into the psychological roots of our dogs' behaviors, acknowledging their ancestral heritage while appreciating the complexities of their psychological makeup. This insight guides us in tailoring our approach to each dog's unique needs, allowing them to express their true selves. The aim is not to alter our dogs' inherent nature but to harmonize our lives with theirs, fostering a symbiotic relationship where both humans and dogs can prosper. It's a journey marked by patience, understanding, and a steadfast commitment to our dogs' well-being. Through this process, we also embark on a journey of self-discovery, confronting our own vulnerabilities, fears, and our capacity for empathy and authentic connection. We then step outside of our human ego and face those issues from our past to move forward and overcome wounding, the painful things that hold us back, and wants that we've falsely identified as needs. Our dogs become more than just mirrors, they reflect aspects of ourselves we often can't see ourselves; they help identify those blind spots we are all too often unaware of, especially when they are urgent issues we need to solve. This journey not only enhances our caretaking of our dogs but also propels us towards becoming more compassionate, centered, aligned, educated, mindful, and balanced individuals.

My experiences, particularly with individuals involved in dog fighting, have revealed that change is possible across a broad spectrum of humans directly intertwined with dogs. Early in my career and to this day, I've worked to dismantle dog fighting operations and educate those involved about proper human-dog guardianship. Although these individuals come from some of the harshest environments, I've aided them through a deep transformation, leading them away from dog fighting altogether. This change isn't quick and it certainly wasn't easy. The inward journey, or soul path, they've ventured to overcome, is a deeply ingrained generational tradition of how they've treated dogs. It's easy to look from the outside and say that dog fighting is horrible, and it truly is one of the most evil things imaginable, but if you've been brought up that way you'd probably do the same no matter how moral an individual you consider yourself. Their openness and willingness to learn and rise above the generational curse is inspiring. No matter who you are or what you've been conditioned to think anyone is capable of turning around and treating dogs with the proper care they deserve. These transformations highlight the potential for positive shifts in the way dogs are treated, irrespective of a person's past.

Transitioning from this reflection on deep cultural shifts, it's important to consider how we, as dog guardians in a more everyday context, can embody leadership and communication with our dog. Contrary to the dynamic many people share with me, where their dogs seem to be in control, dictating their owners' routines from sleep to play, my dogs do not dictate the schedule of our day. They do not decide when we wake up, go outside, or engage in various activities. It's crucial for us to always assume the role of the instigator and initiator, understanding this approach is in the best interest of our dogs. By adopting this leadership, we avoid reacting to every signal as a demand and instead, we must be keenly attuned to what our dogs are truly trying to communicate and what they really need, without misinterpreting their signals through our human lens. This balanced approach to leadership and responsiveness is a skill that all humans in a relationship with dogs need to develop.

This phenomenon begs the question: How have we arrived at a point where dogs are perceived as running the show? Surprisingly, this issue persists even among those who employ negative, dominant reinforcement methods. Attempting to assert control in such a manner paradoxically reinforces the dog's dominant role, leaving them confused about the true leadership within the pack. True leadership is not about dominance or submission but about confidence, competence, and the ability to guide without resorting to intimidation, fear, or aggression. Failure to embody these qualities will lead to dysfunction within the pack dynamic. My approach, especially evident when introducing new dogs into the pack, is grounded in solid leadership and clear, calm communication. This ensures that even with the addition of new members, the group remains balanced and harmonious. The ease of these introductions highlights the importance of a leader who is both respected and understood by their dogs and not someone who is simply giving in to their demands.

It Starts with Us: Understanding Acceptance

Thinking about how we're always chasing the next best thing or something different in all parts of our lives, from what we own to the people we're with, it's interesting to see how this mindset spills over into how we relate to our dogs. We're always looking for more, but this constant search is the complete opposite of simply accepting things as they are. And really, embracing acceptance can change our lives and our dogs' lives in massive ways. Acceptance isn't about giving up. It's about seeing the value in what we have right now, in our situations and relationships, and realizing they're exactly what we need at this moment. This way of thinking can change how we interact with our dogs substantially. Accepting our dogs as they are, with all their unique traits and behaviors, and admitting to our own shortcomings, sets the stage for a real connection and healing.

Starting to live this way, with acceptance, isn't something you can do overnight. It's a commitment for life. It means dealing with our own feelings, like guilt, hostility, or frustration, and making sure we don't dump these feelings onto our dogs. Seeing our dogs' actions, and really, every experience in life, as opportunities to learn rather than problems to fix, can really shift our mindset, leading to more gratitude and understanding. This is how I live with my dogs. I go with the aforementioned 'no schedule schedule,' intentionally varying our daily routines to maintain a sense of novelty and intrigue, mirroring the unpredictable ebb and flow of life in the wild. This approach helps us all learn to be flexible and resilient and reinforces my role as their steady leader and protector. By being consistent and showing them I'm always there, they feel safe to check out new things, knowing I've got their back.

When it comes to interacting with our dogs, the concept of being aware and present is critical. Being there for them, tuned into what they need and how they're feeling without making it about me and my perspective, is the foundation for a trust-filled relationship. This approach deepens our bond with our dogs and changes how we approach life, creating a more peaceful and fulfilling life for us and our beloved dogs.

The way we connect with our dogs often shines a spotlight on our own egos, offering a deep dive into our psyche. You see it everywhere, from the tough streets where having a fierce powerful dog boosts someone's street cred, to a regular day at the park where someone's ego might take a hit if their dog doesn't act perfectly.

Transformation and breakthroughs often occur when we let go of judgment and the compulsion to fit ourselves and our dogs into predefined molds. This shift away from expectations to a stance of acceptance allows for a more authentic and freeing interaction with our dogs and in life, period. Recognizing that the narrative we construct around our dogs' behaviors can significantly impact the reality we create is vital. By focusing on the negative—labeling behaviors as 'bad'—we will inadvertently perpetuate these patterns, both in our dogs and ourselves. The conversation expands to reflect on the broader implications of our behaviors and attitudes, suggesting that our own neuroses and unhealthy patterns can influence how we perceive and interact with our dogs. This reflection invites us to consider how societal pressures and personal judgments shape our relationships with our canine companions. The projection of our inner turmoil onto our dogs not only affects their behavior but also reflects our struggles with self-criticism and societal expectations.

Let's consider the sad story of the orcas at SeaWorld. These incredible creatures, pushed to perform for crowds, remind us of what happens when we impose our will on another living being. The concept of using these majestic animals for entertainment is both alarming and indicative of our flawed perspective on our relationship with nature and its creatures at large. This comparison is directly relevant to our dogs. Just like those orcas, our dogs aren't here to entertain us, to do tricks, or to follow orders every time we whistle. They are feeling, thinking beings who deserve respect. When we start to truly experience our relations with dogs as teachers and companions on our life journey rather than tools to gratify our silly whims and egoic-based desires, we lay the initial foundation for a proper relationship with them.

Many of us naturally long for a peaceful life with our dogs. This isn't just a fanciful wish; it's something we can actually achieve. But it requires us to take a deep dive into how we build trust and respect with our dogs. It goes beyond "training" to forming a bond that's almost telepathic, where a simple look or a subtle movement of our body language energy is all it takes to communicate. This kind of connection isn't about forcing compliance. At its heart, our journey with our dogs isn't about becoming masters of commands but about mastering the art of communication. It is about paying attention to the little things in our dogs' behavior, understanding their needs, and responding in a way that deepens our unspoken bond. This takes time and even more importantly patience. You must have a readiness to listen and learn and a strong desire to improve. After enough practice, you will get to a level of understanding, where you don't need to rely on commands anymore. Instead, you'll have a natural, easy way of communicating that makes the relationship function in an effortless state of flow.

Witnessing dogs turned into something lesser in the name of "training" leaves me disconcerted. Seeing this kind of thing hits me deeply hard, clashing with everything I stand for. It's a clear sign of how our craving for control can twist the beautiful bond we could have with our dogs into something harmful. This realization fires me up even more to push for change in the way we treat and interact with our dogs. It's become more than just a professional goal; it's a personal crusade. I fully endorse promoting methods that respect a dog's individuality, creating bonds based on mutual respect instead of fear, but unfortunately after all my years of experience they don't seem to exist. But this isn't just about dogs. It's bigger than that; it touches on compassion, discernment, and respect that should color all areas of our lives. It's a wake-up call to remember the effect our attitudes and behaviors have on those around us, urging us to elevate our standards and ensure we're acting from the right place for every being we encounter.

The Heart of Responsibility: Deepening Our Canine Bond

When it comes to our responsibility for becoming proper dog parents, we must understand the anxiety in our canine companions is not just about recognizing signs of distress but also about comprehending the depth of their social needs and communication barriers. Dogs, inherently social beings, thrive in a community setting, a family, a pack. This intrinsic need for companionship is not limited to their kind but extends to their human families and even other species, forming a multi-species pack. The concept of a solitary life for a dog is not just unkind; it contradicts their very essence. Dogs communicate in a language rich with nuance and subtlety, a language that, despite our best efforts, remains largely foreign to us. Our attempts to mimic canine communication often fall short, leading to misunderstandings and, inadvertently, to the exacerbation of anxiety and trauma.

The notion that physical dominance or mimicry of dog behavior by humans can establish leadership or alleviate anxiety is profoundly misguided. The human aspect of caretaking for a dog is not about being a dog. It sounds ridiculous but people do try to emulate certain behaviors dogs undertake. For example, the act of grabbing a dog by the scruff, inspired by a misinterpretation of canine interaction, ignores the complex dynamics of respect and understanding that govern dog behavior. Similarly, the practice of forcibly rolling a dog onto its back as a display of dominance not only misrepresents the nuanced language of canine hierarchy but also risks damaging the trust and bond between you. True alpha dogs do not need to resort to force to assert their position; their leadership is acknowledged through subtle cues and deep-seated respect within the pack.

One aspect that we need to focus on when stepping into the responsibility of caring for our dogs is how we interpret their behaviors. Consider, for instance, a scenario where a dog's whining is quickly labeled as 'bad behavior.' This label is not just a misnomer but a glaring oversight of the dog's attempt to communicate. Whining, in the realm of canine expression, is not an act of defiance but a dialogue, a way for them to convey their demands, discomforts, or fears. The question then arises: why are these expressions deemed inconvenient or problematic? The answer lies in our misunderstanding, or perhaps our lack of understanding, of their language. This communication barrier often leads to misconceptions about their behavior, casting it in a negative light simply because it doesn't align with human norms or expectations. It is important to remember that dogs are in fact not humans and we shouldn't put their behaviors into a good or bad box. This is where the concept of acceptance needs to be applied. We need to interact with our dogs in a way that they understand not try and force them to be human or be held to a human standard.

When we communicate with our dogs in a manner they comprehend—through consistent signals, energy, and body language—we lay the foundation for a solid relationship. This bond, unbreakable and resilient, becomes a cornerstone of their well-being, enabling them to navigate the inevitable changes and challenges life presents. It's not about shaping your dog, it's about shaping yourself to be able to understand your dog so that when things change you are prepared. Change, after all, is a constant. For dogs, adaptability and resilience are innate qualities that, when nurtured, can significantly mitigate stress and anxiety. It's our responsibility to ensure that the 'inner mechanics' of our communication and interaction with them are aligned. When these elements are in harmony, the potential for stress or anxiety, triggered by change, is greatly reduced.

It's often said that dogs are humanity's best companions, but this invites us to consider the nature of our interactions with them more deeply. Imagine, for a moment, instructing a dog to do something for us, much like we might casually ask a friend to grab something from the fridge. The idea of issuing such a directive to a friend feels out of place. When we ask a favor from a friend, we do it in a way that's appealing and inviting, not commanding or demanding, because if we were to do so, they definitely wouldn't fulfill it. This underscores how inappropriate it is to treat our dogs in a similar way. It's a less extreme version of what is done to those whales at SeaWorld and it's up to us to make that change.

It hits us that our dogs might be feeling anxious, just like we would if we were constantly criticized or faced with confusing expectations from someone close to us. This thought really drives home how similar some aspects of our emotional worlds can be to those of our dogs. It's our job and responsibility to treat them properly to not cause them any undue level of stress. If this sounds like too mighty a task then companionship with a dog is not within your capacity.

Imagine a scenario where your boss sends you an email late on Friday, hinting at a significant mistake in a project you've been working on, without providing any specific details or guidance on how to address it. The message ends with, "We need to discuss this first thing Monday morning." This leaves you with a cloud of uncertainty and stress hanging over your weekend, unable to take any action or clarify the issue until the meeting. You spend the next two days anxious and frustrated, trying to guess what went wrong and how it might impact your job, only to find out on Monday that the issue was minor and easily resolved. This kind of communication leads to unnecessary stress and a feeling of helplessness since it lacks clear information and immediate avenues for resolution. You'd understandably be quite upset with your boss and that's exactly what it is like for your dog. It begs the question, if we don't like being treated that way, why would we put a dog through it? We need to end the miscommunication and inconsistent signals altogether.

Dogs, with their quiet insight, act as profound mentors, showing us the subtle lessons of life and togetherness without ever uttering a word. But these lessons are only revealed to those who are ready to truly listen, to connect with the unique ways dogs communicate, going beyond mere words. The common but archaic belief that we need to command dogs comes from a basic misunderstanding and, at its core, a fear of losing control. This fear, driven by our own uncertainties, leads us to impose a strict framework of commands, wrongly thinking this will close the gap between us and our dogs. However, in this quest for control, we overlook the true nature of our bond with dogs—as fellow travelers on life's journey.

Our Imperfect Relationships with Dogs: The Responsibility to Show Up Everyday

One of the core responsibilities we must undertake is achieving a flow state. Stepping into the right frequency to cultivate a flow state is about more than just achieving peak performance; it's about aligning with a state of being that fosters deep connectivity and presence, both with ourselves and our dogs. Every day, I catch myself on the brink of losing that centeredness, that equilibrium that connects me to a heart-centered way of living. This world incessantly pulls us towards distraction and disconnection, urging us to live from a place of overthinking and overanalyzing, which only serves to dysregulate our entire being.

In the quest for personal transformation—be it changing our thoughts, behaviors, or lifestyles—many of us lose touch with our hearts, engaging in what can only be described as spiritual bypassing. Yet, the heart's connection to the mind is where true transformation begins. When these are disconnected, we operate from a place of shadow and ego rather than from light and authenticity. This is where our dogs become our greatest teachers. They embody pure divine sources, operating without the confines of the ego, radiating from a space of pure heart—but not in the way humans typically perceive love.

When I practice heart coherence, connecting deeply with my heart, I don't feel love; I experience a profound sense of cohesion, gratitude, safety, protection, and an acceptance, and oneness with the divine. This state of being is not about an overt expression of love but about an intrinsic, deep-rooted unity. Dogs, with their unique spiritual anatomy, naturally exist in this state. They don't need to strive for it; they are inherently profound healers by their very nature. This realization often comes as a revelation to many people I work with. They come to me feeling guilty for not having recognized this sooner, worried about the stress and discomfort they've inadvertently caused their dogs. However, the beauty of this journey is the ability to shift our frequency, to choose a higher level of being and presence every day actively. It's about more than just a fleeting thought or feeling; it's how this elevated consciousness manifests in our actions, our interactions, and our relationships with our dogs. It's not about being perfect but about taking the responsibility upon ourselves to show up for our dogs every day.

Chapter 10:

The Embodied Alpha Leader

Beyond the Badge: Police Dogs' Journey to Home Life

Throughout my career, I engaged significantly with canine units and police dogs, offering a practical application of my curriculum and expertise. I was once called to assist an officer who was retiring and wished for his dog, a partner who had lived exclusively working with the police, to transition into a household companion. This desire highlighted a common issue: service dogs, including those for the blind, for anxiety, police work, or search and rescue, often experience significant stress due to their handlers' lack of understanding of their needs. These dogs have been put into roles where their life's mission was about what they could provide for us humans, which has neglected their own well-being in the process.

The officer, influenced by a machismo belief in his alpha status and leadership, failed to genuinely embody the essence of true embodied alpha leadership. This attitude, rooted in an outdated notion of dominance and control, did not effectively communicate leadership to his dog. Consequently, despite the dog's apparent obedience in the field, it exhibited signs of stress and anxiety, conditions that are not conducive to optimal performance in any role. The scenario underscores the broader issue: stress and anxiety significantly hamper the ability to function at one's best, whether human or canine. Imagining a shift in this dynamic, where officers are educated and inspired to adopt authentic alpha leadership, suggests a profound potential for reducing job-related stress and enhancing performance, a transformation I have witnessed many times. However, the retired officer's dog struggled with this transition. Accustomed to a role defined by the need to be in charge and protect, the dog became overly protective and reactive when introduced to a domestic setting. This behavior, while stemming from a place of loyalty and the instinct to alert us to perceived danger, became problematic due to the dog's heightened stress levels. This experience illustrates the intrinsic protective nature of dogs, one of their many gifts to us. They possess a heightened sensitivity to their environment, often alerting us to danger well before we become aware of it ourselves. However, when a dog's stress is not adequately addressed, this protective instinct can manifest as overprotectiveness and reactivity, underscoring the need for a balanced approach that considers both the dog's well-being and natural instincts.

Faced with a challenging situation involving this dog, known for its potential aggressiveness, I employed a unique approach to address and alleviate the dog's stress and confusion about its role. Recognizing the importance of communication in a language the dog could understand, I devised a plan to demonstrate that the dog no longer needed to bear the protective responsibilities it was not suited for. This process aimed to instill trust in the officer as the rightful leader, thus significantly reducing the dog's anxiety and allowing its true nature as a companion to emerge. The strategy began with triggering the dog's protective behavior by knocking on the door, prompting an aggressive response. Following this, I instructed the officer to lead the dog into a dark bathroom on a leash, enforcing a brief period of isolation (only five seconds). Repeatedly, we implemented this technique, and it wasn't until the 33rd attempt that we saw a breakthrough. This persistence was crucial, as each iteration was a step towards dismantling the dog's ingrained responses and building a new foundation of trust and understanding. The officer's role was pivotal throughout this process, embodying the essence of alpha leadership not through dominance but through calm, still energy—a "lighthouse energy" that's unwavering, neutral, yet supportive. This technique, based on the principle that isolation for a pack animal signifies vulnerability and potential survival threat, was designed to recalibrate the dog's behavior. The isolation method leverages the instinctual fear pack animals have of being alone, as their survival heavily relies on the collective strength and support of the group.

By providing a clear, understandable consequence for its actions, the dog could learn and adapt without harm to its spirit or the human-dog relationship's integrity. The aim was not to punish but to guide the dog towards a better way of behaving that aligns with its well-being and the desired harmony within its human family. The transformation witnessed in the dog, from aggression to trust, proves the effectiveness of this method. It demonstrates that with the right approach, rooted in patience, consistency, and an understanding of canine psychology, we can facilitate profound changes in behavior, reinforcing the bond between humans and dogs based on mutual respect and leadership. This approach benefits the dog by reducing his anxiety and clearly demonstrating what his role is and isn't. It also places the human in a position of confidence and empowerment, fostering an energy that promotes regulation and profound, long-lasting change. The energy invested in or combined with this technique is just as important as the technique itself.

I've encountered situations where individuals, after hearing me on a podcast or different interviews, attempt to replicate a technique I've described, only to apply it incorrectly. They're motivated by a desire to find a solution, yet lack a comprehensive understanding of the method's intricacies. This leads to misapplication, as seen in cases where they don't adhere to the specific timing required for the technique to be effective or where the energy they put in is misaligned, which is just as important. For instance, ensuring only five seconds of quiet when isolating a dog is crucial; extending it to ten seconds undermines the entire process, diluting its effectiveness. This precision is vital for the dog to make the correct association between its behavior and the consequence. The misunderstanding extends to common reactions to unwanted behaviors, such as scolding a dog long after it has forgotten the act, like chewing a valuable item. This approach fails because the dog cannot connect the punishment with the behavior, rendering the scolding not just ineffective but abusive. Similarly, traditional methods of potty training, like punishing a puppy by shoving its face into its mess, are not only misguided but cruel. These actions come out of frustration and a lack of understanding, and do nothing to teach or guide the behavior in a manner that dogs can comprehend.

Addressing, resolving, or transforming behavioral challenges demands a deeper, more nuanced approach than what can be gleaned from a single tip or a video. Achieving lasting change and truly supporting a dog's well-being requires a comprehensive, multi-layered strategy. This is especially true for those seeking to nurture their dogs in the most beneficial manner possible. Even well-intentioned positive reinforcement can be harmful if it reinforces behaviors stemming from a codependent relationship, thereby constituting another form of abuse. What is necessary is stepping into the embodied alpha leadership role and aligning the pack hierarchy for optimal function.

Embodying the Alpha Leader: Transforming Human and Dog through 'Peaceful Dog Mastery

The 'Peaceful Dog Mastery' method holds a universal applicability, regardless of the breed or type of dog you have. Its effectiveness lies in its capacity to first transform the human. This transformation is key, as it directly impacts the well-being and life experience of the dog. At the core of this approach is the concept of the 'Embodied Alpha Leader', a model of presence and energy that I like to describe using various metaphors: a lighthouse, a peaceful warrior, or even a ninja. This embodies a heightened awareness – not one of hyper-alertness, but of being centered, grounded, attuned, clear, and neutral. An embodied alpha leader maintains composure, is never thrown off balance, rooted in a foundation of calmness.

It's important to note that alphas are not just born; they can be made. We all possess the capacity to embody this alpha energy, to show up for our dogs and ourselves in a way that is aligned and heart-coherent. Each person's alpha presence is unique. Some may be more type-A, driven, and edgy, while others may embody a calmer, more nurturing alpha energy. My role is not to fit everyone into a rigid mold but to help them access the strongest, most confident, and heart-coherent version of themselves. This version is tailored to each individual, nurturing and nourishing to their unique personality and spirit. The ultimate goal is to create a setting where dogs willingly trust and follow their humans, driven by genuine respect, confidence, and most importantly out of their free will and choice not because of stress or obligation. Interactions with your dog should never be about force and you shouldn't force your dog to follow you. The goal is for the dog to choose you as their alpha out of their own free will and volition. There is nothing more gorgeous than an animal that has free will and freedom of choice.

A crucial aspect of being an embodied alpha is the ability to handle stress and challenges effectively. It's not about creating a stress-free bubble; that's unrealistic. It's about knowing how to ride the wave of life's stressors and triggers. How one responds and manages these situations defines their alpha status. Instead of crashing into life's challenges, an embodied alpha manipulates the energy to work in their favor and for the highest good of all involved. This entails a balance of heightened awareness and readiness to act without succumbing to reactivity.

The path to peace certainly begins with self-reflection, assessing our thoughts and attitudes towards ourselves, our dogs, and the nature of our relationship. People often fear that embracing 'Peaceful Dog Mastery' requires extensive personal development work. While personal growth is a component, the beauty of this method is its accessibility and immediacy. Clients can start with simple behavioral shifts that immediately impact their dog's behavior. For those who wish to delve deeper, the journey can be transformative, impacting every aspect of their lives. 'Peaceful Dog Mastery' is truly for everyone, adaptable to the depth and intensity of the journey one is ready to embark on.

From Anxiety to Assurance: The Alpha Path to Dog Wellness

Let's explore an example that helps highlight what becoming an embodied alpha leader can do. We've teamed up with local dog sitters, known as "Rovers," to help dogs transition smoothly from shelters. Instead of sending these pups to stressful and toxic boarding facilities, we're placing them in cozy, home-like settings to prepare them for life in a foster home. A recent chat with one of the Rovers shed light on a pretty common issue: a dog named Gem was showing signs of stress, like whining and crying non-stop from night till morning. This situation made the "rover" take a closer look at the best ways to support a dog feeling this way.

Looking into Gem's behavior, she realized that her actions weren't about looking for someone, which is how we might see it. Instead, her behavior was a natural reaction to a bunch of big changes around her, she was accessing who she could trust. More significantly, her adjustment involved being integrated into a human family and environment where no one knew how to communicate in her language. This situation, although managed by wonderfully intentioned and great-hearted caregivers, highlighted the necessity of establishing a confident foundation for her, despite the misunderstandings. It's a classic case of us humans putting our own spin on what dogs might be feeling, often misunderstanding their signals. To help Gem with her anxiety, I suggested to the Rover that they shouldn't respond to her whining with words or touch. Instead, the focus was on sharing calm, supportive energy without saying a word. What was needed, as I recommended, was for the whole family to take on the leadership role, speaking to Gem in a language she understands and meeting her exactly where she needed to be met. It might sound a bit odd at first, but the idea is that engaging with a stressed dog can always make their anxiety worse.

Being an embodied alpha leader is all about presence. It is a state of being rather than a throwaway trend. When interacting with dogs, caretakers need to have a real presence. Dogs are scarily perceptive and giving off the right energy is important. It's similar to when someone can just feel that there is something off or unsettling; it's hard to put into words but the vibe is clear. Imagine you're walking through a peaceful park and come across someone repeatedly checking their watch, looking around anxiously, standing up, and sitting back down at a bench over and over again. They are occasionally making brief, hurried phone calls. This unusual behavior in such a setting might raise your suspicions or concerns, making you wonder if they're dealing with an emergency or perhaps involved in something secretive. In a similar vein, when interacting with dogs, the energy we emit is crucial. When someone interacts with a canine the energy they put into the room is above all else. It can't be denied– it's like the massive purple elephant in the room.

This process not only helps clients improve as caregivers for their dogs but also inspires them to elevate their own lives. Redefining the alpha role from a misunderstood and often negative stereotype to a beacon of excellence, leadership, and personal enrichment allows individuals to break free from conventional views. This strategy isn't about neglecting the dog or their feelings. Rather, it's about establishing a calm, steady atmosphere that reassures the dog their leader is confidently handling matters, allowing them to feel at ease with this understanding. It's incredibly similar to the dynamic between a parent and child. It clicked for the Rover when I made that parallel, that this concept mirrors the idea of not reinforcing negative behaviors in children. And guess what? It worked like a charm. The next picture showed Gem snoozing peacefully, and reports indicated an immediate transformation in her demeanor, proving just how effective this method can be. This whole experience didn't just give the Rover a new way to look at dealing with dog stress; it also highlighted the bigger lesson that our reactions to anxious dogs need to be filled with patience and an understanding of their true intrinsic nature. By embracing this mindset, we're setting the stage for more peaceful and healing interactions with our dogs, helping them navigate through their anxious moments with a gentle, guiding energy.

In my experience with dogs who have faced challenging circumstances, I've discovered a unique method of bonding that supersedes mere companionship. It involves sitting quietly with them, kind of like a shared quiet time, where we are communicating on a deeper level without words. It's about getting a feel for what's bothering them and using intuition to figure out the best way to help them heal. It's a soul-to-soul conversation. When we quiet everything down- the noise, the chatter, the inner turmoil of our busyness we can connect in the most authentic, clear, and direct way- the answers are there for us to receive, we just need to listen in a deeper way. This is where being present, connected, and aware as an embodied alpha leader really shines through. The best part is, you don't need to be some kind of psychic to do this. It's something anyone can do. The key lies in quieting your own mind, welcoming an attitude of openness, and being completely present and caring when you're with your dog. When we do this, we start to understand what they need from us, where they're feeling stuck, and how we can help guide them out of it. It's about connecting with them on a soul level.

A significant revelation for me has been revealed while dedicating moments of silence with my dogs. It's not just about physical closeness; it's about making a deep, soul connection. In these moments of silence, I connect with all my dogs on a more substantive level, looking for insights into their needs and imbalances. This quiet bond fosters a degree of comprehension and restoration that simply isn't achievable through verbal communication or direct engagement. It allows for healthy boundaries to be defined on a fundamental level. When left alone, dogs don't lament our absence but instead embrace solitude, contrasting sharply with common human interpretations of canine behavior. A common issue people have with dogs is separation anxiety, which can affect them to varying degrees. However, this is simply due to the unfair job description they have unknowingly given the dog. If your dog begins to panic the second you leave; it doesn't stem from the human understanding of missing someone. The issue is that the dog believes that they are responsible for you and when you leave they go into a state of anxiety because they believe they can't fulfill their duty to protect you as part of their pack.

Reflecting on a personal experience, I was away from my dogs for a week. Upon my return, their reaction was nothing short of a testament to the trust and understanding we've built. Their calm and welcoming demeanor was a clear indicator of the secure and stable relationship we share. This reaction highlights the importance of maintaining consistency in their life experience, even in my absence. This is the Holy Grail caretakers should strive for and a huge part of being an embodied alpha leader. Dogs should not be overly distressed after you return home. When a dog views you as the embodied alpha leader, they are perfectly relaxed when you leave because they know that you are responsible for both them and yourself. Put simply they know they have everything taken care of. Then they will naturally be relaxed and embrace solitude. Maintaining this equilibrium is a continuous effort, it's like training for a marathon. You need to continue to run every day in order to build up the endurance necessary to complete the race. It's not solely about our actions or physical presence but also about the underlying energy, intention, and mindset we bring to these interactions. By cultivating a centered, present energy, we can tremendously influence our dogs' behavior in a beneficial way, fostering a relationship marked by harmony and well-being. The importance of intentionality and self-awareness in our role as embodied alpha leaders is a lesson that has been reinforced through all my client interactions and insights.

And there's more to consider, like how we use our voices. Dogs can get overwhelmed by all our chatter because they communicate more through body language, energy, and silent cues. Imagine how comforting it is for them when we quiet down and give them a break from all our noise. This silence becomes a peaceful haven for them. It's in these quiet moments that we can really connect with them in the ways they understand best. Becoming an embodied alpha leader is not about stopping all communication; it's about being more mindful and deliberate in how we interact. It's about tuning into the clear, instinctive ways dogs communicate, understanding and respecting their natural ways of expressing themselves. This leads to a more synchronized and effective connection. By integrating these approaches, we're not just aiding in their recovery; we're building a stronger bond and embarking on a shared journey of growth and healing.

It's essential to highlight the critical roles that learning and comprehension play in our relationship with our dogs. This book is designed to aid those aspiring to improve their rapport with their dogs. However, if people are not committed to comprehensively grasping their dog's essence and absorbing the wisdom contained within these pages—and, more crucially, from their dogs themselves—then the potential for transformation remains unfulfilled.

Moving from the foundational need for understanding, we pivot to the essence of trust in the canine-human bond. Creating trust with a dog isn't a straight path; it's more like making a complex dish with various ingredients and steps that all add up to the final magnificent result. Some readers might prefer a direct, hands-on approach, focusing on changing behaviors to get a different reaction from their dog. For those ready to explore further, there's a path to a truly profound, even spiritual connection. This level of understanding and fulfillment is within reach for everyone who truly commits to the process.

My approach is designed to be flexible, and suitable for both practical needs and deeper explorations. It's about seeing our dogs' behavior as it truly is, without the labels society might put on them or outdated ideas. This change in mindset creates new possibilities that can go beyond just our relationship with our dogs but grow to effect change in areas of our lives we wouldn't have even thought about. In short, the "secret" to transforming our relationships with our dogs isn't really a secret. It's a choice to improve our ability to understand and connect. There are many paths one can take on their life journey. If you want to bolster your relationship with your dog you must follow the path to becoming an Embodied Alpha leader.

Non-Attachment: Expanding on the Principle of Acceptance

Embracing non-attachment doesn't equate to a lack of care or affection. Take my contemplation over my book, for instance. Do I cling to its success? What if it fails to come to fruition? Clinging to outcomes, such as the success of a book, can lead to distress if things don't align with our hopes. Yet, pouring passion and a transformative vision into our endeavors is distinct from being bound by them. This distinction is equally pertinent in our relationships with our dogs. Non-attachment enables us to cherish and tend to our dogs without being caught in the web of unrealistic expectations or dependencies. This will ultimately lead to unmet expectations followed by negative emotions such as disappointment and failure.

The beauty of non-attachment lies in the liberation it grants both us and our dogs. It untangles the often-convoluted mesh of emotions and anticipations, allowing for a more serene coexistence. By releasing our grip on our expectations of our dog's behavior and our own, we embrace a state of acceptance and freedom. This mindset is about acknowledging the present as it is, which naturally eases accumulated stress, and sets the stage for transformation. Non-attachment extends the principle of acceptance discussed in the prior chapter, advancing it a step further.

The principle of non-attachment opens the door to a world of possibilities, sparking creativity and relieving stress. It invites us on a journey to let go of unrealistic expectations that have become second nature. Serene mastery encapsulates the true nature of embodied alpha leadership. It transcends notions of control, dominance, or positive reinforcement aiming instead to foster an environment ripe with trust and peaceful coexistence. It's about ensuring your dog feels protected and at ease in your company, a feat achievable only through a peaceful, non-attached, yet profoundly aligned stance.

Alpha Harmony:
The Essence of Peaceful Dog Mastery

Many people struggle with the concept of embodied alpha leadership because they try to intellectualize it, losing sight of its essence. Leadership in the context of our relationship with dogs is felt rather than thought through. Dogs live in the moment, responding to the energy and presence we project. They do not overanalyze their environment but react to the cues and leadership we provide. This immediacy of presence and action is something we, as their human counterparts, must strive to embody. From the moment I wake, I lead by example, initiating the day's activities on my terms, yet always with an awareness of and sensitivity to my dogs' needs and responses. My approach varies—sometimes my dogs share my bed, other times I sleep alone—but the constant is the clear leadership that guides our interactions. This flexibility does not confuse them; rather, it strengthens our bond, as they trust in my leadership regardless of the day's specifics.

The beauty of embodied alpha leadership is in its transformational effect on our relationship with our dogs. It fosters a state of flow where interactions become effortless, marked by a profound connection and mutual understanding. This state of being, where leadership and companionship blend seamlessly, is the essence of peaceful dog mastery. It's a dynamic every dog lover aspires to—a relationship characterized by joy, fulfillment, and an indescribable sense of connectedness.

In the quiet moments of our daily lives with our dogs, we find the purest expressions of connection and leadership. Consider a simple, yet telling moment when one of my dogs approached me and gently licked my toe twice. In this seemingly small gesture, there's a world of communication. Instead of immediately engaging with her, which might have implied that she was steering our interaction, I chose a different response. By not reacting in the moment, I wasn't ignoring her but rather communicating in her language, maintaining the balance of our relationship. This subtle choice was significant. Her action wasn't a demand for attention or an inquiry about our roles; it felt more like a gentle display of curiosity. By respecting this moment without overt engagement, I reassured her of our bond and her autonomy. What followed was a beautiful testament to her trust: she comfortably lay down on her side next to me. In the language of dogs, this posture of complete side relaxation is a sign of ultimate trust and vulnerability, a state they rarely display unless they feel entirely at peace. This contrasts sharply with the prone position many dogs adopt, especially those trained with a focus on control. Lying on their stomach, they're poised for immediate action, a state of readiness rather than relaxation. This distinction is crucial in understanding the essence of true leadership versus control. In a relationship based on mutual respect and understanding, a dog's relaxation is a sign of trust.

Reflecting on these interactions reminds us that leadership in the context of our relationship with our dogs is about more than just who's in charge. It's about fostering an environment where trust, respect, and understanding allow both humans and canines to thrive. It challenges the traditional narrative of dominance, proposing a model where leadership is about guidance, support, and the freedom to express vulnerability. The foundation of this dynamic begins each morning. Before the day begins, I engage in a practice of heart coherence and meditation, connecting deeply with myself and then extending this connection to each of my dogs. This isn't merely a routine but a profound act of setting intentions for the day, prioritizing the emotional and spiritual bond between us. Even on the busiest days, this practice is non-negotiable, for it shapes the quality of our interactions, ensuring they're rooted in presence, mutual respect, and genuine connection. I'd like to emphasize that it is not a time-consuming practice. It can only take a few seconds or a few minutes to achieve. The more that you practice this ritual the more it becomes natural. This is the desired result; you want to step into a more optimized state of being. This approach to living and leading with our dogs is a lesson in authenticity and truth-seeking. It's a daily reminder that the essence of our relationship should always be evaluated. Through this lens, every day becomes an opportunity to practice living with intention. There is always room for improvement and it's important to not get bogged down by past mistakes.

The Unending Journey: Learning and Loving with Our Dogs

A memorable story from my decades of experience springs to mind. It is a journey from despair to empowerment in the realm of dog companionship. This narrative centers on a remarkable client who, prior to our collaboration, found herself essentially confined within the walls of her condo, a prisoner to her circumstances. The source of her captivity? Her three dogs, whose distress manifested in relentless screaming and howling the moment she stepped out, left her trapped by their anxiety and the ensuing backlash from her community and neighbors. The situation escalated to the point where neighbors' frustration materialized in the form of snarls, stares, and, most tangibly, nasty notes left on her door, each message a testament to the collective unease stirred by the dogs' vocal torment. Thankfully this was not where her story ended; she underwent a complete metamorphosis due to her understanding and approach to this pursuit. Through her dedication and the transformative work undertaken in our one-on-one work together, she realized a profound truth: our journey with our dogs isn't aimed at a specific destination but is a continuous path of growth, healing, and breakthroughs. It's about the process of up-leveling not just our dogs' lives but our own, embracing every challenge as an opportunity to deepen our understanding and connection with these beings we share our lives with.

This narrative mirrors the broader odyssey of personal and soul work, a theme that resonates deeply with my own reflections as I approach a personal milestone. Just as I celebrate the strides made in my own journey, I recognize the infinite potential that lies ahead. It's a never-ending well of growth, learning, and joy, underscored by the belief that there's always more to discover, more to improve, and more to cherish in our relationships with our dogs. This story serves as a powerful reminder that whether dealing with a senior dog nearing the end of its journey or navigating the challenges of behavioral issues, the essence of our bond with our dogs is defined by the space we create. It highlights the spectrum of engagement available to us, from addressing specific stress-induced behaviors to embarking on a profound journey of self-discovery and reinvention. In embracing this path, we realize that being with our dogs transcends mere "training" or working with them—it's about being committed to a journey without a final destination, but filled with endless moments of discovery, bond, and transformation.

Conclusion

In essence, the heart of cultivating a serene companionship with our dogs fundamentally rests with us, the humans. This journey towards becoming a master of peace alongside our canine companions isn't a testament to achieving flawlessness or absolute perfection. Rather, it's an acknowledgment of the continuous path of growth and evolution within our relationship. It's about taking each day as it comes, with a commitment to living out the principles of releasing rigid expectations.

The concept of expectations plays a significant role here—holding onto strict notions of how our dogs should behave only serves to distance us from the true essence of our relationship with them. It's common to find oneself fixated on categorizing a dog's behavior, yet this approach misses the core issue. When our dogs behave in ways that puzzle us or seem out of character, it serves as a direct reflection and prompt to reassess our own state of being and how we interact with the world around us. Our dogs, as mirrors, reflect our emotional and psychological states back on us through their behavior. Thus, every moment of unexpected behavior from our dogs is not just a challenge but an invitation—an invitation to introspect and adjust our own attitudes and actions. It's crucial, therefore, to approach this journey not with self-judgment or labels such as guilt, shame, or a clinging to what we believe should be. Embracing acceptance, and perhaps for some, this notion may seem daunting at this stage, has the power to transform our relationship with our dogs in a profound way. This is the magical elixir for a successful life experience, period.

One particularly memorable transformation involves a client who, alongside her two shepherds, embarked on a transformative journey over the past year. Initially, the atmosphere in her home was one of palpable stress, with the dogs' anxious behaviors creating a cycle of discomfort that extended to them avoiding leaving the house with them. This situation, understandably, strained all aspects of their lives. However, through dedicated effort and engagement with the principles we explored together, remarkable profound transformations unfolded. The pivotal moment came after a coaching session we shared. My client experienced what can only be described as a profound shift in perspective. She reached a place of deep acceptance for both her current state and that of her dogs, moving beyond the confines of labeling their behaviors as either 'right' or 'wrong,' 'good' or 'bad.' Instead, she embraced the reality of their situation with an open mind. She recounted waking up the following day feeling as though everything had transformed. It was as if a veil had lifted, revealing a clearer, more harmonious path forward. The taxing stress of viewing everything from the perspective of right and wrong or good and bad is derived from inaccurate societal programming. It is difficult to free yourself from this programming since it's been ingrained in us.

This breakthrough can be likened to a spiritual awakening, illuminating the essence of freedom within the relationship she shares with her dogs. This narrative underscores the importance of remembering and honoring the sacred bond we share with our canine companions. It's about engaging with our principles and pillars of practice consistently, for mastery in this domain is achieved through daily dedication and a steadfast commitment to supporting ourselves and our dogs authentically. For my client, this realization brought a sense of liberation from societal expectations and judgments. She found herself in a state of complete acceptance stepping into the embodied alpha role, which allowed her and her dogs to enter a flow state of existence together. Witnessing this transformation was deeply moving; it epitomized the essence of Peaceful Dog Mastery. This is not merely about navigating life with our dogs with ease but about reaching a harmonious flow state that encompasses the entirety of our being and our shared experiences with these remarkable animals.

A Call to Action: Join the Peaceful Dog Mastery Movement

After journeying through the pages of this book, you stand at a pivotal crossroads, equipped with the insights and understandings to fundamentally transform your relationship with your dog. The path from here is rich with opportunities for deeper exploration and application of the principles you've encountered. Whether it's engaging with me directly through one-on-one coaching, diving into the immersive experience of the master class, or embarking on the comprehensive journey offered by our upcoming course, your next steps are crucial in solidifying your commitment to peaceful dog mastery. The course we've envisioned goes beyond the foundational knowledge shared in this book; it's designed to be a hands-on, in-depth exploration that not only deepens your understanding but also equips you with the skills to effectively implement these practices. This unique educational journey aims to culminate in a certification, acknowledging your dedication and proficiency in fostering harmonious relationships between humans and dogs.

To embark on this transformative path, your immediate action is simple yet profound: visit peacefuldogmastery.com and sign up. This initial step is your gateway to a world of resources tailored to support you in deepening your connection with your dog. By signing up, you're not just gaining access to exclusive content and programs; you're joining a community committed to the principles of respect, understanding, and genuine love in human-dog relationships. This call to action is more than an invitation; it's a challenge to step into a role of leadership and advocacy within the realm of dog companionship. By choosing to delve further into the world of peaceful dog mastery, you're not only enhancing your own life and that of your canine companion; you're contributing to a global shift towards more empathetic, informed, and respectful interactions between humans and animals. The journey doesn't end here—it's just beginning.

The moment a reader reaches out to share how "Peaceful Dog Mastery" has reshaped their life and the life of their dog, it will be an affirmation of the journey's worth, a profound testament to the impact of steadfast dedication to a vision contrary to mainstream narratives. This feedback will be a source of immense fulfillment and inspiration, a clear signal that the efforts, challenges, and moments of doubt along the way were not only worthwhile but necessary for this revolutionary shift. For me, such responses will serve as a deeply moving acknowledgment, touching the core of my passion and commitment to this cause. It will symbolize the culmination of a journey marked by perseverance, a journey where every obstacle was an opportunity to reaffirm the commitment to a truth I've seen transform lives right before my eyes, now poised to ignite change on a global stage. The realization that "Peaceful Dog Mastery" is not just a book but a catalyst for a global movement is both humbling and exhilarating. To hear that it has changed so many lives is to know that the message of compassionate, understanding, and respectful companionship with our dogs has resonated and taken root. It's a validation that choosing to walk this path, to shine a light on a more harmonious way of living with our canine teachers, was not only the right choice but a necessary one.

This isn't just about personal fulfillment; it's about witnessing the dawn of the peaceful dog movement, a collective shift towards understanding and living out the principles of peaceful dog mastery. It signifies that being a practitioner of peaceful dog mastery is more than adopting a set of rules; it's about embodying a philosophy and a way of being that champions respect, nuance, and genuine connection, thereby contributing to a broader, more profound change. In essence, the feeling of knowing the book has deeply changed lives is a reflection of the broader transformation it seeks to inspire—a world where humans and dogs interact in a state of mutual respect, autonomy, understanding, and love. It's a confirmation that the peaceful dog mastery movement is alive and growing, propelled by every reader, every dog, and every story of transformation. Together, we are not only acknowledging the invaluable lessons these grandmaster teachers impart but also paving the way for a future where the bond between humans and dogs is celebrated as a profound source of wisdom, joy, and mutual growth. A mass awakening is upon us, one by one we can revolutionize the world as we know it. This is the true fulfillment of the journey: the realization that together, we are creating a legacy of peace between humans and their grandmaster teachers.

SCAN HERE